A N L A F ' S   E R G

A N G L E Z   A R K E

Richard Skelton is an artist from northern England. Since 2005 he has produced a series of musical recordings and books that engage with the hidden histories and ecologies of specific landscapes. *Landings* is a collection of texts for the West Pennine Moors of Lancashire, UK, drawn from various sources, including historical treatises, maps, parish records, census data and the artist's own diaries, notebooks and essays. The book obliquely documents his use of music, writing and photography as means of 'colluding' with the various agencies of the land: the seen and the unseen, the heard and the unheard, the 'real' and the imaginary, the living and the dead. Originally published in 2009 as a modest 96-page book, *Landings* has grown over the ensuing years as it attempts to record, transcribe and archive the voices of the here and now, the lost and forgotten.

BOOKS BY THE SAME AUTHOR

Field Notes (Volume One) (2012)*
Moor Glisk (2012)
Limnology (2012)
Nimrod is lost in Orion and
Osyris in the Doggestarre (2014)
Memorious Earth (2015)*
Beyond the Fell Wall (2015)
The Pale Ladder (Selected Poems
& Texts 2009–2014) (2016)
Towards a Frontier (2017)
The Look Away (2018)
Dark Hollow Dark (2019)

* *with Autumn Richardson*

LANDINGS

RICHARD SKELTON

XYLEM BOOKS 2019

Richard Skelton, *Landings*
First published in 2009 by Sustain-Release Private Press
This edition copyright © Xylem Books 2019

ISBN: 978-1-9999718-5-4

Cover image:
'Little Spinner', Georgia, USA
by Lewis Wickes Hine, 1874–1940
National Child Labor Committee collection,
Library of Congress, Prints and Photographs Division

Xylem Books is an imprint of Corbel Stone Press

Landings : Valley of the Small River (2009)

Landings : Names. Dates. Genealogies. (2011)

Word-Hoard (2015)

Chemical Memories (2019)

Appendices

Lancashire Dialect Terms

Farm Names from Census Records

Farm Names from Cartographic Records

The Book

Notes

Index

for Louise Skelton

1975–2004

LANDINGS

VALLEY OF THE SMALL RIVER

2009

ANGLEZARKE

A spur of eastern hills, 1,000 ft
high projecting into the centre. The
greater part a high moorland, 2,792
acres (167 of inland water). There
is no village of Anglezarke, but a
hamlet called White Coppice lies in
the north-west, and another called
Hempshaws in the south-east.

Approaching this outcrop of trees, the atmosphere hits me forcibly. The pitiable nakedness of the boughs and branches. The sudden murmuring of the wind. *Colluding.* I want to make some kind of gesture. An offering. A mark of passing. And to leave it here. Tied to the land.

THE COPSE AT THE BROW
OF SCHOOL HOUSE LANE

How to begin writing this down? Shall it be a simple inventory? A list of parts. Names. Dates. Genealogies. Sound begetting sound. Endless melody.

If I were to say – a robin sings in the trees across the field from this coppice – would that be enough? Could you flesh things out from such a meagre outline? Or should I describe its song? Onomatopoeia. But the bird has long fallen silent before the words begin to form.

And what of the other sounds – the constant polyphony?

> Distant hum of motorway traffic.
> Delicate rattle of leaf against branch.
> Everything in between.

I fill the page as best I can, replace the diary under a stone, and retrace my steps down the darkening lane.

But as I walk back under the eaves of those trees, I ask myself – could any film, recording or photograph tell you this? That whilst I dwelt within that wooded chamber, listening to those brief glimmers of song, I forgot about her, the river and its promise.

All that mattered was without weight or consequence. Nothing lingered or resonated beyond the instance of its own making. Everything listened.

A MEADOW BELOW NOON HILL WOOD

A sheep corpse lies near the fenced borders of a pine plantation. Just one of many I've seen in recent months. The eyes are gone. Always the eyes first. But what half-light breaks now, through those wretched hollows? What tenure now held in other places? Nearby, a body of metal fencing lies discarded in a rusted coil. Something more than proximity binds these things together. Perhaps when that fleshy corpse has long surrendered to the moor, this metal one will remain? A marker for something. An oblique form of testimony.

NOON HILL WOOD

I quickly leave the meadow behind and climb the narrow stile which grants access to the plantation. Pausing briefly on the threshold, I glance along the first row of trees, and then back at the field below. A moment of transition. Passing between worlds.

> *Dark throat of woodland.*
> Craw of pine, spruce and beech.
> Gargling the water that runs
> from Noon Hill Slack.

I last came here in the promise of the year. Sloshing up the small stream and the steep banks. In its higher reaches the trees gather closely together, and the light is dammed by their outstretched branches, occasionally flooding through the gloom in brilliant flashes. And here and there are clearings. Great pools of sky. Natural amphitheatres.

I originally came bearing musical instruments. Now I bring recordings made on those first, tentative forays. Gently bowed strings. Concertina drone. Bird clamour. The sound of leaves and water.

Bringing this time and that time together. Returning the music back to its birthing chambers.

> Hearing it drift, thick, across
> the dark earth. Taking root.
> Brushing against leaf and moss.
> Gathering in the shivering treetops.

And the wood listens to itself.

THE GREY BIRD

It's early. Not quite day. The moor beneath Grange Brow is sodden and treacherous after a night's rain. Thick clouds hang heavily. Morning seems deferred. Suspended.

Why am I compelled here, before this ashen landscape? And there it is again. Distant, but powerful. A summoning call. Travelling the bank of black trees that points north-east towards Turton Heights. Across Hill Top and down Grange Brow. Circling this meadow. Drawing everything together.

Dark threads of song. Muscle. Blood. Bone. All towing the line at the threshold of something. A stark, two-note refrain, unaccompanied. Punctuating the silence. *Calling. Over and over.* Never answered. Removed from hope. And beyond dementia.

the constant polyphony

THE BOOK

And not just moor and woodland,
but the bones of old dwellings.
That somehow people thrived
here, once – perhaps a century
ago. Made these once-proud
monuments that now prostrate
themselves. Elbowing their way
into dirt.

And for some reason, shrouded
like the ruins themselves, an
anonymous archivist decided to
mark them down.

A private book of records.

Inventories.
Observations.
Epitaphs.

Type-written elegies from a
dimly lit past.

The date read 1936.

SCAR TISSUE

A farmhouse. Long fallen into ruin. One of many that litter these moors like scar tissue. Each a fragile testament to a half-forgotten history. Tenaciously clinging to a wind-ravaged existence. Gradually succumbing.

Many of these places have names. This one is called Old Rachel's. A host of questions hover around that name like the wild moorland birds I disturbed the first day I came here.

From *the book:*

> Partly standing in October 1936. A large open fireplace with ingle-nooks. A stone porch to front door with seats. Built lengthways into the side of the hill.

And then in pencil:

> The barn, built on the end of the house, was a large one.

Followed by more typing:

> Was occupied in 1841 by Roger Brown, who was churchwarden. Old Rachels and Abbotts were inhabited until about 1910.

Accompanying these descriptions are two pathos-inducing photographs, presumably taken by the book's author, showing the farm in its first stages of decay. In all, a meagre epitaph for such a place as this, which, even now, in its degraded state, seems to act as a pivot about which the moor wheels.

Later research turns up another photograph, taken in the 1890s.
The farm's last occupants, the Evans family, pose outside. A woman
in white stands just outside the entrance, hands on hips, head
slightly cocked, looking squarely into the camera. A girl crouches
beneath the window cradling an infant, almost receding into the
wall itself. She looks downwards, as if expressing her reticence
to be involved in this depiction of rustic domesticity. And last
but not least, all but hidden by a wall, a young man stands, arms
folded. A century's passing has since transformed this building
from family dwelling into desolate ruin, home only to occasional
wild birds and the sound of the breeze through the Yarrow vale. A
century of collapse, decay and gradual surrender.

And as I clamber over wood and stone, trying to trace its perimeter
– to distinguish it from the moor which threatens to engulf it – I
dislodge bits here and there, unintentionally becoming complicit
in the process of decay. And how to stop the rot? How to salvage
something from time's passage? How long before the map makers
decide to erase this structure completely? Before it becomes a
nameless ruin? And then a mere pile of stones. Mossed over.
Forgotten. How long until they lift its name from their charts and
from our collective memory?

The only thing I can do is fill the place with music.

> To pour sound between wood and stone.
> Into each fissure and fault-line.
> Like rain on an April morning.

But sound, too, falls into decay and eventual silence. Perhaps a
fitting medium for such a commemorative gesture?

And just like the dissolution of this once well-delineated structure, the sounds of my bowed steel strings spill outwards. They cannot be contained. Fixed. Charted. They ripple across the moor. Losing shape and form. Accruing ghostly, shimmering overtones. Mingling with the sound of larks high above me, and the shrill dissent of curlews from across the river banks. An elegy born from stones, dirt and grasses.

Yarwe Earwe Yarewe

edge   brow   moss   heys

delf   flats   clough   lowe

ditch   shore   hill   slack

ford   pasture   height   fold

brook   moor   stake   meadow

CHILD

From census and parish records:

> SP, daughter of JP and EB, was born on _____ 1865 in
> Anglezarke. She appeared on the census on 2nd April 1871
> in Anglezarke. The address was Lower Hempshaws Farm.
> On 2nd April 1871 she was a boarder in Anglezarke. She
> appeared on the census on 3rd April 1881 in Anglezarke.
> The address was Lower Hempshaws. On 3rd April 1881
> she was a farm servant in Anglezarke. She died of drowning
> in a canal on _____ 1887 in Lancashire. She was buried
> in _____ 1887 in Rivington, Lancs. The address was
> Presbyterian Chapel.

More than these ghosts of buildings, the litter of sheep corpses, or
the bones of grasses. More than skin and heather. *Names. Dates.
Genealogies*. And this hovering, imagined presence.

And for some reason I think of Niépce's sun writing. Bitumen.
Lavender oil. Pewter. Those first, eight hour exposures. The sun
making a near-complete transit of the sky. Families of shadows.
Acres of rest.

CODA

Along the borders, the high moors and unminded meadows. Mired in the earth and its green machinery. Meikle's forgotten children. As obsolete now as the flesh they disinherited. Chaff amongst chaff. Stunted. Leg-ironed. Bound to nothing.

But rattle their cages and something still stirs. A harrowed chorus resounds across the moors. Guttural coda to the song of a lost industry.

moors like scar tissue

THREADS ACROSS THE RIVER

Standing in the wreck of Old Rachel's, I look out across the expanse of moorland that bridges the ruined dwellings of Simms and Hempshaws.

More notes from *the book:*

> Said to be a corruption of Helmshaws. Had been a fine barn.
> House may have been two joined into one. Remains of a
> small close planted with trees which may have been a garden.
> There was a hamlet of Helmeshawes in 1566.

Two joined into one. Something about that phrase clings. I feel a weight. A burden. Pulling, choking. Why do the words of this nameless archivist persist in my thoughts? A restless voice from the past. Why am I drawn to follow in the same footsteps? Becoming complicit in something I don't understand. A reluctant successor.

And what do they commemorate, those words, my words? Remains. A poverty of stones, barely distinguishable from the all-encompassing moor. I remember reading somewhere that there wasn't always heather, sedge and moor grass here, but a hay meadow over a century ago. How quickly things return to wilderness.

Taking up a stone from the rubble of Old Rachel's I make for Simms. It's hard going. Or rather, it's soft going. Soft, wet and treacherous. The various tracks, particularly the well-established ones, transform themselves into streams, ditches or mires at a moment's notice. Several times I'm stranded and have to backtrack, but gradually I progress downwards, and begin to dimly hear the sound of the river rising to meet me.

I finally make it to the river side. There's a small wooden foot bridge, possibly 12–15 feet across. It's unmarked on the map. Half a mile upstream – my more usual crossing – there's a small flat stone, about four feet long, which bridges the gully through which the River Yarrow flows. By contrast, that meagre stone structure receives two epithets from the map makers. On the Rivington side of the river is written the word *Ford*, and on the Anglezarke side, *FB* (Foot Bridge). An indication of status? Antiquity? Popularity?

Down here, a little further up from the wooden bridge, is a large stile which offers a good view of the meeting of two rivers. Although of comparable size to the Yarrow, Green Withins Brook isn't named on the contemporary 1:25,000 Ordnance Survey map. They seem to be of similar length – the Yarrow being born at Hordern Stoops by Will Narr, and Green Withins Brook just below Redmonds Edge, by Standing Stones Hill.

The sky has noticeably darkened since I arrived here. It feels close, this stretch of land. Hemmed in. The bridge. The confluence. The dark grey waters flecked with foam. A place of neglect. The narrow wall that borders the Yarrow on one side seems to accentuate the natural geometry like a scar. It's time to leave. I make my way quickly up the steep banks and reach the ruins of Simms as the rain begins to fall. I place the stone from Old Rachel's amongst the others and look back, barely discerning its dim, languishing shape across the moor. A glimmering thread – a filament – now binds these places together.

As the rain intensifies, I look around and see a wooded area on the brow of the hill above me. Minutes later I'm breathless, crouching in the dark under rows of conifers as the weather spends itself. From the eaves of this wood I look out and see the plantation on the lower slopes of Noon Hill. Shelter belts of trees. Conifers ushering in alder, rowan, birch and oak. I remember collecting fallen alder catkins and oak leaves amidst the pine cones last March. My name for that place is Noon Hill Wood, but it isn't marked on any map. A place on the threshold of things. Uncertain. Still becoming.

I look inwards and all is dark, dense and close. Row after row of sullen larch. Many lean in with roots exposed. And here and there are clearings; fallen trees, piles of branches and earth. I shelter beneath the roots of one fallen tree, but it's too oppressive. Taking a small tangle of loose roots I make my way back outside. In the open air I see a kestrel skim the perimeter of the wood, hover on its threshold, and swiftly fly away.

something more than proximity

Will Narr, [1,175]

Spitlers Edge, [1,286]

Redmonds Edge, [1,230]

Standing Stones Hill, [1,083]

White Ledge Hill, [1,030]

Counting Hill, [1,066]

Black Hill Lower, [1,083]

Round Loaf, [1,076]

Black Hill Upper, [1,138]

Great Hill, [1,250]

Brown Hill, [1,030]

Cold Within Hill. [919]

names dates genealogies

DISMANTLED

Hollinshead Hall. A wreckage situated in the shallow valley between Great Hill and Cartridge Hill. I read that it was dismantled after it fell into disrepair in the late nineteenth century. Its masonry was then reused to build houses in the nearby village of Belmont, and the network of dry-stone walls along Darwen and Longworth Moor.

The more I reflect upon this, the more Hollinshead becomes a complete entity again, albeit in an exploded form. It didn't diminish. Rather, it became assimilated into the surrounding landscape. Transformed from one state to another. Solid to liquid. The law of the conservation of matter. Neither created nor destroyed.

I wonder if Old Rachel's was ever dismantled? And those other farms at the head of the River Yarrow? Perhaps my act of transferring small stones from one ruin to another can be seen as a transformative gesture, motivated by the need to experience these places removed from the connotations of death and decay? No longer, then, these isolated ruins, etched with pathos and loss, but something more ambiguous and powerful.

LINES OF FLIGHT

I watch a solitary crow
follow the Yarrow upstream.
Tracing its own river in the sky.
Higher, much higher, gulls wheel
and meander, bicker and squabble.

Could I know the landscape
without ever seeing it?
Limn its ghost, mirrored
in these intangible paths –
these lines of flight?

I WANTED TO TELL YOU

I wanted to tell you about the river.
Its lymphatic grace. Its capillary beauty.
Devourer and devoured.
Predator and prey.

But the river is dumb to tell me.
These tricks of the light.
This grazing incidence.
A silvering prism.

A MANDATE

Following the Yarrow downstream. It occurs to me that I'm drawn
as much to the river as to the ruins that prostrate themselves
along its banks. From its headwater at Hordern Stoops it traces
a pathway between Hempshaws and Stoops, Simms and Old
Rachel's, Wilkinson Bullough and Brown Hill. Pulling them into
a mesh of connections. Setting them in opposition. Binding them
together.

But more than proximity and geometry, the Yarrow and these
ruins are bound up in a darker history. Between 1868 and 1877
the river was dammed further down the valley, forming a new
reservoir to help meet the increased demands for drinking water
by the swelling populations of nearby towns and villages. In doing
so, two farms – Turners and Alance – were submerged; the latter
perhaps reconfigured into the bridge which now bears its name.
The Yarrow Reservoir wasn't the first of its kind in this area – three
others (the Anglezarke, Upper and Lower Rivington Reservoirs)
were built by the Liverpool Corporation between 1850 and 1857.
It seems as though the flooding of valleys to create artificial lakes
was something of an epidemic in the mid-19th century, but in
comparison to some regions, where entire villages were inundated,
the inhabitants of Anglezarke and Rivington emerged relatively
unscathed.

So why did most of the farmsteads in the surrounding area
become vacated over the next 30 years? The answer may lie with
the Liverpool Corporation, and its mandate to provide clear
drinking water for its city's inhabitants. At the turn of the 20th
century it attempted to acquire the watershed land surrounding its
reservoirs with the reputed intention of demolishing all buildings
in the vicinity, including Rivington village. A clear indication
of the metropolitan mindset. The homes of the rural few were

expendable. They constituted a contamination threat to the purity of an entire city's water supply.

William Hesketh Lever, owner of the Rivington estate, had other ideas however. Something of a philanthropist, he wished to bequeath it to the people in the form of a public park. On the 8th of August, 1902, an Act of Parliament was passed, which, amongst other things, granted Liverpool Corporation the right to 'acquire certain lands for the protection of their Rivington water supply'. The Rivington estate was duly sold to the Corporation, but not without condition. Lever Park was enshrined in the legislature 'for the use and enjoyment of the inhabitants of the county borough of Bolton and generally of the public for ever'. Moreover, the village of Rivington was spared, but this protection sadly didn't extend to the adjoining lands of Anglezarke, then owned by a Mr Percival Sumner Mayhew. The Corporation acquired the Anglezarke water-catchment in 1904, and although clause 19.3 of the Liverpool Corporation Act made provision for Mayhew's exclusive right to shoot (grouse and pheasant) on Anglezarke's moors, no mention was made of the tenant farmers – of their right to tenure.

As Gladys Sellers noted, in her essay 'The History Of Anglezarke Moorland Farms', tenants' leases were annually renewable. Evictions weren't necessary. Who could withstand the will of a corporation? Within three brief years the remaining farms on watershed land were vacated. Did the corporation demolish the buildings shortly thereafter, I wonder? A safeguard against their future habitation? Or were they simply left to dereliction and decay?

SOURCE

To the source of the Yarrow.
Along the sheep tracks and broken walls.
Through the long grasses, the meadowsweet and the cuckoo spit.
If I spent enough time by its banks, could I get to know the river?
Its rapid tracts. Its sudden lulls.
Its changeling colour. Its constant cold.
If you placed me along its length, blindfolded, could I tell
you where, just from its sound?
Would that be enough?

ANGLEZARKE 1901

47 Males 46 Females

22 Households

RUNNING A LINE

From *the book:*

> He stated that the stones which formed Brown Hill were
> removed to make or repair one of the reservoirs. The
> contractors running a line and bogeys to carry stones.

It's a compelling image. Running a line. A physical connection
between two places. An act of transference.

As with Hollinshead Hall, so with Brown Hill. And how many
others, I wonder? Clearly there's a practical, logistical motive
behind the impulse to dismantle these buildings and reuse their
raw materials elsewhere. But there's an unintended resonance
which is felt, still, all these years later. A sensation that these once
discretely proportioned dwellings have become transfigured,
extended – incorporated into a sprawling lattice of earth, air, water
and stone; filaments in a weave of interconnecting threads.

The landscape is a catalogue of movements. An inventory of
pathways, visible and intuited. A table of the elements, endlessly
reconfigured:

Hovering along the kill paths of kestrels as they bisect the Yarrow
valley. Trembling in the haze of the red road that runs at dusk
from Simms to Wilkinson Bullough. Straining in the summoning
call that tightens over Grange Brow and Folds Pasture. Gathering
in the shivering tree tops of Noon Hill Wood and Holts Flat.

And yet, could it be that my efforts to collude in this hidden
geometry – this phantasmagoria – are rooted, not in nature, but
in the charts, plans and inventories of civil engineers? When I
move stones from one ruin to another, am I unwittingly following

the edicts of Town Hall? Carrying out the will of corporate government? I wonder what happened to those forgotten pragmatists who shaped the modern topography of Rivington and Anglezarke – Hawksley, Cubitt and Rendel? Their legacy is writ large in clay, pitch and stone, but their names are lost – buried beneath the very waters they convened to create.

And what about Thomas Duncan, architect of the Yarrow reservoir, who died before its completion? Was he sensible to the rippling consequences of flooding this valley? Was there a moiety of tact and consideration given to the naming of these new structures? Turner's Embankment and Alance Bridge. Each a deference to what had gone before? A gesture that stressed continuity and perpetuity, rather than disruption and transience? Or perhaps something which originally evolved out of public sentiment had by then become formula and procedure? No need to think of a new name, just take what's already there.

But should I be so eager to censure the likes of Duncan, and his successor, Joseph Jackson? Aren't they simply part of the continual process of transformation? Agents of change? Architects of progress? And haven't I benefited from their endeavours? Aren't I unwittingly complicit in all this? After all, the fresh, clean tap water that I have always taken for granted flows directly from this river – from this reservoir. And although I've done my share of manual labour, I've never worked the fields, herded sheep or operated a loom. Am I qualified to comment? Is my sympathy little more than patronage? Would my sanctimony on behalf of those who once lived here be welcome? Regardless, I feel a debt of gratitude is owed; their homes were sacrificed for my future benefit – for my convenience.

But more than anything, it's the here-and-now – these remnants – to which I feel connected. Despite my desire to view them as part of a continuum, it's difficult to ignore the feelings associated with abandonment and decay. And given my personal history, it's all too easy to view this landscape through the prism of bereavement. To discover loss wherever I look. To conjure sorrow from dereliction, pathos from crumbling stones and rotting wood.

But then again, perhaps I should embrace such emotions? Does the burden of grief bestow certain rights? By becoming death's witness, does one also make a kind of transition – an Orphic journey – and become attuned to certain voices? Over these last few years I've slowly made my passage through this landscape. Limned the edges of its streams and rivers, followed the contours of its hills, the eaves of its woods. And to what purpose? With whom am I colluding? Who are my guides? What name did this place have before records began?

Looking out over this expanse of impounded river water, I try to imagine the former valley. What must it have been like, over a century ago, in the shadow of the industrial north? (The legacy of the enclosures – landless tenants scratching a living. The repeal of the Corn Laws and the constant threat of poverty. The dawn of cheap mass-manufacturing and the ensuing decline of cottage industries.) The census records from 1841 tell the story all too plainly. Families were large and many shared dwellings with each other. Children were put to work as soon as they were able. The Marsden's of Wilkinson Bullough had five children, three of whom worked as weavers, including Ralph, who was just seven years old. Nearby, at the old farm of Simms, Charles and Jane Holt also had five offspring, including Alice, whom the census records describe as a 'winder', aged ten years (possibly at the nearby Lister Mill).

And when children couldn't be employed at home, they were often packed off to live with another family. I think again of SP. Born in 1865. Boarder at the age of six. Serving girl at sixteen. Living on the high moor with someone else's family. The river and the old hay meadow. What imaginings of a future life? Dreams of escape to the nearby cities of Liverpool or Manchester? Spires and columns on the dim horizon. If only the dry-plate system had been perfected earlier, then there might have been a photograph. A face for a name. But there are no chemical memories here.

SOUNDS OF THE MOOR

In some oblique fashion this music has come to work its way into the moor itself. Played over and over again at various times and places, it mediates my experience of this landscape. Conjures it. Summons it. Suffuses it.

Bowed, plucked and chafed steel strings. The sound of stones gently rubbed together. Soft soil sprinkled on resonant wooden bodies. Grasses and leaves intertwined around neck and fretboard. Bone and wood plectra. Sound folded on sound. A collusion of place and instrument.

calling over and over

HOLLOW (REPRISE)

False plane.
Hollow.
What caused
your loss of heart?

The dull
incessant roar.
Duress.
Commuted metal.

Sing
the air's engines.
Lichen
memory.

The sum
of all knowledge.
Withered.
Forgetting.

GREEN WITHINS BROOK

It's April, but spring's becoming has been prematurely halted.
Buried beneath wreaths of thick snow. In March I saw curlews
by Bromiley Heys. Later that month, I began to hear them in the
pasture by Moses Cocker's. Their stark, elegiac cries suffused the
ghosted landscape.

Today a solitary lapwing traces impossible patterns in the sky.
Tumbling. Diving. Stitching invisible threads across Noon Hill
Wood and along the meadow towards Shore. A dizzying but futile
attempt to sow the seeds of spring in this winter moorland. And
the blanket of snow amplifies the merest sound, such that I can
hear the fizz of the bird's call, like the crackle of spent fireworks,
before the more customary glissando.

Later I cross the Yarrow by the ford and walk beyond Hempshaws,
up towards Standing Stones Hill. Somewhere between here and
Redmonds Edge is the source of Green Withins Brook – the
stream which is devoured by the Yarrow near the ruins of Simms.

On the far side of Great Hill lies a place called Cold Within Hill.
Surely then, there should be a *Green Within Hill* somewhere
hereabouts, from which the brook should rightly flow? Or perhaps
'Within' has the sense of 'withe' or 'withy', meaning willow?
Green Willow's Brook? It's not hard to imagine, especially given the
connection between willows and weeping, tears and water.

With these thoughts in mind, I begin the walk up from the icy
track between Hempshaws and Simms. A climbing, stony path
quickly dwindles into a rutted trail, made treacherous by snow
drifts. Time after time I fall, as the deceptive blanket of snow gives
way to unexpected depths.

Finally, after nearly losing my concertina to the brook itself, I stop and resign myself to failure. I'd hoped to play at the source of the brook, but I'll have to make do with a place by its banks. I kneel by the fledgling stream and suspend trembling drones above its surface. They seem to hang in the air, amplified, long after their natural resonance has decayed, as if mimicking winter's extended tenure in this sleeping landscape.

CAGED

Blood and the facial disc.
Noiseless. Unmoved.
A bright crest of optic nerve.
Against my dull eye and the hovering dark.

Keep watch the bruised horizon?
Watcher? You? Of fur, quill and bone?
Amongst the stone and fenced remnants.
Along the banks and the black fields.

Tiny palpitations. Filaments of life.
Hidden dramas of shade against shade.
And my senses are wretched. Caged.
Whilst you cage the sky.

YIELD

Come down by the banks of the river. Place your hands in the water. And hold them there. Slowly let the cold take you. Close your eyes and yield. And just as this river has found its way into the landscape, century over century. Find your hands and arms between rock and stone. Find your place through touch and instinct. And I promise that just before the pain becomes unbearable. Before your body begins to shake uncontrollably. A deep stillness will wash over you. And you will forget. And by the banks of the river. The pain will slowly, imperceptibly subside. The gift of stillness will gradually pass. And your muscles will move again.

CLING

Unrot. Cling. Withered, bloody inks. Phlegm and glimmer.
She looks downwards. Centuries of the river's chatter. Tracing
its perimeter. Phials of snow. Some kind of gesture. Families
of shadows. Transits of the sky. Scenting the bones of grasses.
Bowed, plucked, chafed. *Clamouring*.

A FITTING GESTURE

I think back to my early attempts with sound. And even then.
Sound made tangible. Physical. Not a disturbance of the air, but a
viscous, healing liquid.

> To pour sound between wood and stone.
> Into each fissure and fault-line.
> Like rain on an April morning.

But it strikes me that the most apt and fitting gesture is one which
requires no premeditation. One which I've made many times,
instinctually. To touch. To hold. To feel. I remember a quote from
Paul Eluard, describing his wife Gala: 'Her body is the shape of my
hands.'

It strikes me that the only way to know this place is through touch.
To place myself inside it. Incorporate myself into its compressed
landscape. To reside, for a while, within its shattered rooms.
Its deserted chambers. To allow my arms and hands to become
extensions of its oblique geometries. Gently plug holes and fissures
with my own body. To feel it. Observe the impression left upon my
skin by its obdurate contours. To bear its scars, clinging like kisses.

more than skin and heather

these tricks of the light

CUCKOO

Who wrote Anglezarke?
The river, all mouth and
chatter, dries up. The
blabbing fields cry wolf.
Sheep stare blandly. In
the glib darkness I held
the moor in my hands.
Rolled it up in circles.
Conjured it from my
pillow. But now the
night eyes of the wood
glower. The moor turns
its back. Disowns me.
*You come here but we
don't need you. Begone,
cuckoo.*

SEEMED

it seemed to shake
to stir for a moment
(but for a moment)
and the sully of cloud
seemed to lift
from its back
and the sun

BRINGING IN THE MAY

A week of hot weather has finally ushered in spring. Blossoms. Verdancy. Fecundity. There's an old fertility rite called *Bringing in the May*, which involves decking the outside of dwellings with May blossom. It's a custom that has probably long since died out, but there's still some vestigial superstition surrounding haw flowers. Not too long ago, for example, it was considered extremely bad luck to bring them indoors – the act somehow presaged illness and death – perhaps due to the smell of the woodland hawthorn, which is said to resemble rotting flesh.

But the smell in the air today isn't hawthorn. As I make my way through the borderland between the moor and the reservoir, I pass at least half a dozen lamb corpses. The moor on the other side of the wall is full of ewes with lambs, and as the wall is too high – and there are no gaps or passages – I can only think that these dead animals have been unceremoniously dumped here. Out of sight, out of mind. Literally passed over to the other side.

We might speculate that the sight of them decaying in full view causes distress to mothers and siblings, or upsets the delicate sensibilities of passing ramblers. Whatever the reason, there's a certain fittingness in their occupying the liminal ground between moor and water – markers along the slopes of a drowned valley – a place of transit and transformation. And their rapid evisceration by the landscape's various agencies somehow recapitulates the decay and surrender of the moorland farmhouses scattered hereabouts. Everything is subject to the same laws of birth and death. Nothing remains untouched.

MIRROR

A lone foxglove grows between
two collapsed roofing beams.
Nettles gather around the blasted
fireplace. Masonry lies covered
in a lattice of lichen and moss.
Beetles, ants and woodworm
thrive in natural litter. Tiny specks
of bright fungus trace contours
along rotting timber. And as
I follow these contours, they
seem to recapitulate those of the
surrounding hills. A grey mirror. A
subtle echo. Question and answer.
You in me, and me in you.

OF THE LAST GENERATION

Found. A dog-eared paperback. Essays on local history. And amongst them, these few paragraphs on the old farms:

> A branch road leaves the lane near here going northward to four of the old farms, now fast crumbling to ruin. The first farm served by this road was Stoops, a small farm near a bend in the brook. A little further on the opposite side was Old Rachel's, a much bigger farm with a good stone water trough filled with cool clean spring water, and among the buildings we find a doorstep made from an old cheese press stone, which is a very good example. Then we go to the right and over the brook by an easily seen ford, to Higher and Lower Hempshaws, both once prosperous farms.

> Immediately above these two farms is a field of about five acres entirely surrounded by a tall stone wall now falling into decay. This field was the 'lambing croft' where ewes were brought in severe winters, when lambing would be a difficult problem on the open moors, to have their lambs in comparative comfort and safety.

> The valley of the small river hereabouts was described as the hamlet of Helmshawsyde in a document dated 1520, and the earliest mention of the spot is Elmshaw about two hundred years before. This earliest name describes the valley here as a small one where elm trees grow. There are none here now but I remember some years ago coming across a mock orange tree in full bloom in one of the old gardens, and just behind Old Rachel's a farmer and his sons made their own bowling green in the nineties of the last century.

The children of the last generation of farmers here are now approaching old age, and I have often talked with them about their life on these lonely farms. They would never agree that the life was lonely. One told of going from here to join the army in 1914 on the outbreak of war, and after seeing service in Egypt, France and Mesopotamia, he came home in 1919 to find his parents living in Horwich and the farm empty and desolate. Another story was of the young son of one of the farmers being told by an aged farm labourer to go quietly over one of the fields on the moor edge, because a lot of brave men are buried there.

From *About Rivington* by John Rawlinson, 1969.

BY THE BANKS OF THE YARROW

the river's wound and
the staunching light

a reach of water and
night's inks

bleeding into
nothing

HORDERN STOOPS

A kestrel limns the vast banks
of mist that coil around the
lower slopes of Will Narr.
Arrow. Rough hill. *Faierlokke*.
The rowans are bearing fruit.
Raspberry canes in the old
garden. Migration differentials.
The curlews are long gone, but
swallows fatten themselves over
the old hay meadow. I can hear
voices by the masts of Winter
Hill. Families of shadows on
the moor. Bitumen. She died of
drowning. A small, shallow dell.

fallen	flutter	flown	swell
leaf	last	wing	whir
fur	blood	clot	scar
wire	bark	gape	sky
hand	veil	wool	clay
stream	back	brick	wound
feather	tide	river	down

UNDERTOW

Standing in the ruins of Parson's Bullough I place a marker by the nettled stones. Taken from a facsimile of *the book*. Another epitaph:

> House demolished. Probably used for building the Yarrow
> Reservoir, 1868–1875. Barn in good state of preservation
> and in use.

As the shifting half-light briefly traces ghost tracks across the fields, I look out towards Alance Bridge and the mouth of the Yarrow, retracing its course back up the tree-lined channel towards Anglezarke Moor. And somewhere far up there. Beyond sight. Old Rachel's.

I suffuse this place with the sounds recorded at that ruin, near the head of the river, many months ago.

> Stones dislodged from a bitter and brittle dam.
> A well of music and memory.
> Alluvium and fragments of melody.
> Stirring in the flood waters.
> Finally flowing downstream.

The Yarrow. A conduit between these two places.

And looking out across the reservoir, its placid surface shivers. A shadow of undertow. As the river unburdens itself.

VOICE OF THE BOOK

More and more, words from *the book* come to me, unbidden.
Fragments. Unconnected. Untethered.

>—A corbel stone over the barn door.
>—The house has gone.
>—Raspberry canes in the old garden.
>—A complete ruin in 1936.
>—The date read 1649.
>—The stone edging of a flower bed.
>—Some land on the Noon Hill side.
>—Found overgrown with turf.
>—Referred to in 1765.
>—Two joined into one.

But not a riddle, begging to be solved. Or a series of clues, pointing
to something. Instead, like the call of that grey bird. Simply there.
A presence. More real than the landscape.

The heather. The cotton grass. And bracken. And the wind. And
those words, over and over. Two joined into one. A hideous
murmur.

Two joined into one.

OFFERING

It's been over a year since I left an offering here. A little box. Music. Photographs. Sense memories. I cross the spoil heap towards the outcrop of trees. The soft earth underfoot. Faint memories of that first visit, with her, many years ago. I try to remember my reasons for secreting these things here. *A mark of passing. Tied to the land.* Something to hold against the forgetful earth. And its hideous, healing softness.

And just as the soil quickly absolved our first footprints, so this copse has forgiven my subsequent intrusions into its sanctified chambers. Benignly mending the broken twigs and branches that marked my clumsy trespasses, and wrapping itself in a thick, impenetrable veil of vegetation. If my motive for returning was to rediscover that commemorative gift, then I've been thwarted by these wreaths of fresh foliage.

I sit on the threshold of the copse. Grasp handfuls of balsam leaves and thread them into the sound hole of my mandola. Rub their greenness onto its dull brown strings.

It strikes me that this process has been more about letting go than leaving a mark. That there was a kind of lesson, here, in this wooded marshland.

Amongst the branches and balsam, with the sound of crows overhead.

ANGLEZARKE 1911

37 Males 26 Females

13 Households

THE STAIR ON THE MOOR

There is a stair on the high moor which overlooks Black Hill and Counting Hill. The narrow stone causeway which winds its way over Redmonds Edge suddenly drops into a shallow, water-filled ditch, before climbing steeply up the bank on the other side. Many of these waterways act as natural drainage systems on Anglezarke Moor, although some – such as Devil's Ditch – are perhaps ancient, man-made earthworks. Eventually, much of the water here will filter through peat and stone, along channels and gullies, before draining into Limestone Brook, and from there into the Yarrow.

Always the Yarrow. I visualise the water's journey down into the reservoir. Threads. Moorings. Similitudes. Recalling the Yarrow's great stepped bye-wash, and the standing water in its lower reaches, I look around me, at this miniature – a small stone stair rising out of a dark, stagnant pool. I hold the connection in my mind for a moment, as the morning's flickering rays illuminate the intervening landscape. Water, stone, earth and air. And these shifting spasms of light tracing patterns back and forth across the moor.

SCRIPTURES

Rain has made the field treacherous this morning. I gently remove the diary from its wire carcass. Sodden. Bloated. Obscene. Like the fresh sheep corpse at the entrance to the field. It's as if the book is taking on the form of its surroundings. Its once precise, rectilinear proportions are bowed and warped. A lump of rotten wood fetched up from a stream. It flops open on an empty page. Fine tracery of silken filaments. Rain water percolated through rust wire. Gauze of dirt and mould. Should I add my own marks to these oblique scriptures? It belongs less to me than to the field now. What will become of it, I wonder?

BECKONING

Along the old lane that skirts the slopes of Rivington Moor. Glimmering tracery of ice and stone brocade. And on the horizon, the silhouette of Noon Hill and its tumulus. Later, as I walk back along the ice road, I find myself glancing back. Something in the alignment of those places. The road. Its lattice of fencing. The hill and its contours. And the darkening sky. And somewhere beyond – the ruins of Coomb, Old Rachel's, Stoops and Hempshaws. Distant, hidden, but nevertheless present. And even though the cold is bitter now, and there's barely any light – these geometries, visible and intuited, somehow compel me. Fasten me to this place. Or rather, they beckon me to find my place amongst them.

FIRMAMENT

She was with me. We were walking down the old pathway. It was
quiet and I heard her shallow intake of breath. She was looking up
and I looked up. I saw nothing, and then I saw them. Hundreds, it
seemed, high, high up in the firmament. They seemed to multiply
before our eyes. The sky, sick with them. Metal. Burning. I felt her
hand grip my arm, trembling, and tasted blood in my mouth.

EPITAPH

A girl crouches beneath the window. The bird slowly beats a track high above the water's edge. This earliest name describes the valley. Its shattered rooms. As if expressing her reticence. Along the banks and the black fields. I carry this river. And the offices of the dead. There is no village. Names. Dates. Genealogies. They cannot be contained. Fixed. Charted. A meagre epitaph. As I clamber over wood and stone.

FROM AN UNMARKED RUIN

Towards an isolated phalanx of trees. Framed against the horizon. There are ruins here, too. Smothered in barbed wire. A disembodied sheep skull presides over this place now. I play for a while; small stones, twigs, feathers. Trying to get this place and my instruments to collude.

Later that day I scour the maps and records. So many forgotten. I hadn't realised there were so many. A handful endure, subsist, even thrive, but there were once so many. And their names were earthed to the moor:

Coomb	Keck	Grut
Cliff	Brinks	Moor Edge
Rough Lee	Gills	Clump
Stone's House	Higher Knoll	Gir' Nest

Or they spoke of apparent wealth, opulence and the concomitant desire for longevity. That self-aggrandising gesture – to erect a monument. To bequeath a legacy. Something that will endure:

Albion Villa	New Temple	Scott Hall
Calico Hall	Pall Mall	Solomon's Temple
Lyon's Den	Pendennis	Sour Milk Hall
The Lords Hall	Peewet Hall	White Hall

But mostly, they spoke of antiquity, and of a name, tied to a place:

Old Brooks	Old George's	Old Isaac's
Old Kate's	Old Knowles	Old Lord's
Old Rachel's	Old Thatch	Old Will's

Names that linger even now, beneath thin wreaths of soil and vegetation, waiting to be unearthed. But why these names, and how did they become rooted here? A collusion of propriety, tradition and superstition, or something altogether more elusive?

LET SLIP

Are you there now, child? A soft voice among grey stones. *Yarwe. Earwe. Yarewe.* Black river. Knife gleaming on the moor's whetstone. Keep the path between Higher and Lower. The hollow tree and the old garden. Blow your hands to keep them warm, child. Blow among the embers of Helmshawsyde. Blow the sparks of names in the sky above this shieling. *Andelevesarewe. Anlauesargh. Anlewesearche.* Let slip, quiet fury of the moors against dumb forgetfulness.

there is no village

RAPTURE

Does Anglezarke end with Spitlers Edge? Sure enough the parish
boundaries lie there, but what about the other side? From Sharples
Higher End to Higher Anshaw, High Shores to Bromiley Pastures.
And the silent ruins of Naylors and Pimms. To whom do they
belong? How are names fastened to places? Do they chafe at the
tether, become unmoored, catch in grasses and along walls, snag
and tear? From the basin of Belmont to the heights of Will Narr –
the litter trail of a name caught in different places:

> —Hoar Stones Delf
> —Hoar Stones Brow
> —Horden Butts Delf
> —Hordern Pasture
> —Hordern Stoops

Attrition. Atrophy. Change. Written into the landscape. And
did the nearby farm of Stoops get its name by the same process?
Association by proximity?

From here – this no man's land – I can see Great Hill, and behind
me, Cartridge Hill, and running between them, the old turnpike
road.

Crows cough and wretch somewhere above me. Through the
trees I watch a wind-hover suspend the earth beneath its wings.
Weightless. And a solitary car cuts through it all, making its journey
past Piccadilly towards Belmont. For half a minute after it is gone,
I can still hear its engine on the road.

Last year I came here. Crossed the darkening threshold of the
wood. On this day, I lingered within its silent precincts. What
marks remain? Why does it matter? I look around, foolishly

searching for some remnant. A tangible link to strengthen the memory. I remember, back then, enacting a private ritual, suffusing the wood with the quiet sounds recorded at that cordate ruin, Old Rachel's farm.

Trying to knit those places together, to draw a thread across the frayed borders of the landscape. To rewrite those boundaries – to annex this place, drawing it into the other. *Two joined into one.*

Today, all I have is a dictaphone, which I hang from a tree before venturing further into the wood. When I return, I replay the sounds it has gathered, fancifully imagining that I can hear a faint trace of that melody played here a year ago. Something written between tape hiss and leaf shiver, mechanical whirr and the calls of distant birds. Something and nothing. A rapture for the membranes of the ear.

PARIAH

Breathe quietly. Become motionless. Lose your identity to the
mass of stones and nettles. Finally it will come. Bird totem of these
outcast ruins. Pariah, whose hated shape is written in the biotic
memory of all small things. (I remember watching a bored, solitary
crow harry the falcon across the fields. The victim screeched its
protest as the black bird forced it, weary, to ground.) And here
it comes, gliding the bank of the narrow stream. *Tinnunculus.*
Pivoting, effortless, as it suspends the moor on ferrous wires.

Suddenly, Great Hill and Ratten Clough make sense. The quiver
of its wings and the arrow of my blood. Its bristling senses spark
across the moor, making a late-September fire out of the dim
embers of summer.

And long after its presence has been extinguished by the
encroaching dark, I remain, looking for a trace – a flint for the
memory – amongst the heaped, broken stones:

> —Coil of barbed wire and string
> —Fragment of moss-fastened vertebrae
> —Thistle seed head and stalk
> —Bone of small animal
> —Mottled feather
> —Curved section of roof tile

Matter for the construction of song. Ingredients for the medicine
bag. Thing-poems of the moors. Vesch. Synecdoche. Sense map.
Connective tissue.

EMBERS

Uncovered. More words on the old farms. Written over a century ago. Families. Histories. Origins:

> Who first gave the name to Old George's is not known, and in a
> like manner Old Kate's memory has died out.

> ...

> In the Middle Ages the name of a tenant was often handed down
> from one generation to another as describing a certain farm or
> holding which had once been identified with the name long after
> all connection between the two had ceased.

> ...

> These farms, no doubt, stand on the site of homesteads once
> occupied by the early Rivington freeholders, the Knolls and the
> Gamelsleghs, but both these families died out so early that it is
> difficult now to trace their exact connection with Rivington,
> and they take us back to such remote times that they fail to rouse
> interest in the mind of the ordinary reader, however much they
> attract the antiquary.

The all-too-brief survey concludes with these remarks:

> It is, perhaps, hardly necessary to apologise to the reader for these
> few notes on the old farmhouses, but the spirit that regards only
> castles and parks as suitable subjects for historical research is not
> dead, and so perhaps one should say something in self-defence.

> Fifty years ago history was regarded merely as a means of handing
> on records of the acts of kings and emperors, and chronicling the

doings of great generals in war and bloodshed. Today a better understanding is abroad, and the study of court intrigues is left alone while men ponder on the silent growth of a nation, and students delve into the past to see how our laws grew and our customs were formed.

We are slowly beginning to realise that every village on our countryside is a kingdom in miniature, and that each homestead may enshrine a story – if we but trouble to unearth it – as full lessons for those who will read them as the history of a mighty castle or a king's palace.

From *A Short History of the Township of Rivington…* by William Fergusson Irvine, 1904.

I wonder what Irvine made of his contemporary landscape, and the upheaval that ensued from the building of those reservoirs, which saw the majority of the old farms vacated? Despite his assertion that 'each homestead may enshrine a story', the voices of those farmer-tenants who endured remain tantalisingly silent.

My thoughts turn again to John Rawlinson, who – some sixty years later – exchanged stories with the elderly sons and daughters of the last generation of farmers. Gently blowing over the embers of memory. Reviving that dwindling connection with the land itself. But now, nearly half a century after Rawlinson first published his recollections for posterity, himself aged fifty or more, I wonder if the coals have permanently grown cold? Has that connection, born from word of mouth, and passed from person to person, become irrevocably severed?

Yet perhaps it's in the breach that these things become

transformed? Absence. Bereavement. Yearning. The imagination recoils from a vacuum and seeks to fill it. Divorced from their context, lists such as these churchwardens' accounts have an almost poetic quality:

> 1782 — John Wilcocks for Finch's Land.
>
> 1787 — Will Latham for W. Burton, 'Garnets', Anglezark.
>
> 1840 — W. Woods for Old Cates.
>
> 1841 — Joseph Heyes for Roger Brown, 'Old Rachels'.
>
> 1844 — James Bain for Old Knowl.
>
> 1845 — James Bain for Nightingale's, Anglezark.
>
> 1852 — I. Bain for Turner's, Rivington.
>
> 1854 — I. Bain for John Winstanley, 'Gir' Nest', Anglezark.

The span of years lends beauty to that which was once banal. Could this explain why I haven't approached the current tenants of those few farms that endure, even now? Moses Cocker's, Bradley's, Wilcock's, Jepson's, High Bullough and Siddow Fold.

But aren't their stories worth telling? Don't their names also merit the dignity of being written down for posterity?

a flint for the memory

thing-poems of the moors

GONE

The grey bird is gone. Its cry no
longer frames the captive landscape.
The curlews, gone. Their birthing
halls deserted. The watcher, *aderyn
corff*, is absent. Blended into nothing.
Swifts, vanished. (In May, as I inched
along Sheep House Lane in a violent
gale, a swift rose up beside me, sails
switching, seeming to share for a
moment in my private struggle. Its
arrow, I thought, had been blunted.
Its scythe notched by the stony
weather. But then it lurched forward,
effortless, through a fissure of its own
making, leaving me stranded, seasick,
head reeling.)

And here by the path on Hoar Stones
Brow, I find a large, black feather.
Crow rudder. The only testimony –
on this blank morning – that the air
bore something on its back. Lifted
high on its shoulders. Singing.

AUTUMN

A century's passing and the listening
rattle. Crows bicker in the trees
overhead. Rhymed leaves. Dew grass.
Wing skirr. Engine. Siren. Machinic
murmur. Threads across the river.
Collective memory. Left to nettles
and to barbed wire.

FALL

By Stronstrey Bank I watch birch
leaves fall. Hurst Hill. Black Coppice.
Autumn's sickness. And the old
pathway, the grey stone and its glib
markings. And the red road at dusk.

MIMESIS

There is a purpose here.
Following the bend
of this small, nameless
stream, my steps invoke
the path of the Yarrow,
miles away, as it tumbles
down from Will Narr.
Mimesis. The knots
of my hands and the
knuckles of ash above.
Joints. Junctures. Cross-
ings. An arboreal sweep
of collarbone. And
beyond the blood river.
A musculature of hill
and meadow.

ANGLEZARKE 1921

25 Males 26 Females

10 Households

MADE

Who made Anglezarke? I watch the wind-hover clutch the air above me. Does the bird stoop and kneel to the earth? (Countless times I've watched it fall from its ledge in the sky). Or does the earth, its play thing (that dull orb beneath it), rise to meet those open arms, like a child to its mother?

ON SAMHAIN

We are not on the old paths, by the road's edge or the boundary fields. There are no alignments, markers or signs. We are not amongst the sacred or the derelicted stones. No lights are fit for us, and we linger where we fell, or where fell things broke us. And although our tenure is passing, we are ever here, and ours is the moor, this shieling, this *ergh*. We watched the birthing of this river, and every night is a festival of the dead.

RIVER SONG

What have you given, that you have not already stolen? Flaunted desolation. Made your woe-songs in dull chambers, with dull strings. But our song is the river, the song of all deaths, the song of passings. At night you came, and we prepared a pathway down to the water's edge. But you clung to that which you must return, and lost yourself in the black fields. And now Autumn flounders and casts leaves into the swirling air. Will you ever return?

NAME

Though you are not here, and were never here, can you not feel
it? Winter, calling each in, blithely gathering? Marking your
place amongst us. Hill and bone. Skin and heather. A memory is
nothing more than this. Nothing more than touch. Pressed forms
in the cold, grey earth, and the river, ever yielding.

But these wrote words you hold against the circling seasons.
Regret, loss, leavings. Marks on the skin. Unknow them.
Listen, instead, to Winter's promise.

Come down by the banks of the river.
And I shall teach you the secret name of things.

I sat by the banks of the river, with the
moor rising up behind me, and my words
ran dry. And yet these letters lingered in the
dust of another's thoughts:

Give me a box of silver birch,
something light and easily burnt,
but don't enclose me
airless in earth; I belong to the moor
the miles of bracken and heather
I've been a prisoner long enough
now let me be wherever
the changing wind blows me.

Phoebe Hesketh, 1909–2007

A Box of Silver Birch by Phoebe Hesketh, 1997.

And all the while
a voice, an answer,
rippling across the
moor:

Look, I carry this river
my hands are its banks
my arms its course
and I love.

The river and its promise.
Without weight or consequence.

You passed me on the church road. Did you not see me?
Dusk. The engines. Your eyes. *Colluding*.
Last year I came here. Do you not remember?
They drowned this valley. She died. Drowning.
I found her in a handful of stones.
Do you think of me? Still?

but where will remains
these remains will

lasting in defiance
of the years

which fall
wingless on earth

I turned and looked
for you becoming light

I turned and looked
for you becoming

and what impression
the shape leaves

Footprints. In the soft, damp earth.
Mine encircling hers. How quickly
they faded into barely recognisable marks.
Had we really been here at all?

LANDINGS

NAMES. DATES. GENEALOGIES.

2011

SOMETHING UNRESOLVED

It has been a long time since I last ventured there. I resolved not to return unless I could trace a path from my door to one of the seventeen thresholds that grant access to the moor. I wanted to connect – with footfall – the place where I resided and the place where I wished to be.

As days turned into weeks, and weeks into months, I devised more elaborate and self-defeating ways of investing this process with meaning. If I were to walk there, then I would do so only across fields, along hedgerows, streams and ditches. I would avoid tarmac and concrete, marking out instead a natural corridor – a map of the green verges that criss-cross the intervening landscape. The distance was perhaps only 5 miles as the crow flies, but how tortuous was the route that involved no roads? Did such a route even exist?

In the weeks leading up to this resolution, my encounters with the landscape had become increasingly elaborate, demanding, oblique.

I kept a vigil for as long as I could in the field above Old Rachel's. I lay motionless in the long grass from where I could see nothing but sky. In the absence of visual stimuli I resorted to cataloguing sounds.

> Whisper of grasses against my ear.
> Clack of stonechats, perhaps twenty feet away.
> Needle-song of a lark, high in the sky above me.
> Engine noise of a car climbing the hill past Moses Cocker's.
> Roar of the M61, softened to a murmur by the distance.

After several hours I observed a kestrel glide above me. It lingered, hovering for a few seconds – perhaps trying to comprehend this foreign shape beneath it – before moving on, following the blazing scent maps of mice, voles and other small things.

Towards the end of my days there, I felt compelled to spend a night on the moor. I stood in the tall grass and sedge above the ruins of Stoops farm, watching my dim shadow lengthen as the moon rose behind me, high above Winter Hill.

A night of exhilaration, of boredom and terror, in which the merest of sounds took on other forms – grew large in the expanse of darkness. After several hours the sheep gradually stopped calling to each other from across the river banks, and a brittle quiet descended. More than anything, I wanted to walk down to the water's edge. *To see the black river in the moonlight.* But a mixture of fear and reason kept me locked along the safe paths high above.

As morning approached I watched a faint blush spread along Redmonds Edge to Spitlers Edge. When the sun finally rose above Will Narr there was an audible reflection in the valley, a cacophony of song, a rejoicing.

But what was the purpose of encounters such as these? Each felt like a test which I was bound to fail, or a show in which there was no revelation, no dénouement. If I was searching for an epiphany, a conclusion, then it was too subtle for my senses to apprehend.

Over the half-decade during which I visited Anglezarke, I felt increasingly lured to the yellow-brown precincts of Holts Flat and Sam Pasture, the green-black chambers of Noon Hill Wood, the pale seats above Will Narr and Great Hill. In the late spring of 2008 the cottage at Dean Wood House, overlooking the Yarrow Reservoir, became available to rent. I made tentative enquiries, but the asking price was more than double what I could afford. With so few dwellings in Anglezarke, it seemed that my desire to reside within that landscape – to simply dwell there – would never be fulfilled. This event, which seemed relatively insignificant at the time, in retrospect became a kind of turning point. If I couldn't live there, I would forever be a visitor. An interloper.

In this light, it strikes me that there was something desperate in those last gestures, those final offerings. An attempt to cling to a place in spite of circumstance. Acts of devotion. Of love. If I had continued with them, where would they have taken me? And to what end?

The previous summer I remember searching for the ruins of Calico Hall on the high moor above White Coppice. I veered off the path between Coppice Stile House and Grimes, and came across another ruin unnamed on contemporary maps. The building (called Heapey Moor farm, I learned later) had all but collapsed, but in the remnants of a small outhouse I found a collection of waterproof matting carefully folded under a large stone. The roof of the storehouse had been fixed with a large black plastic bag, which, now tattered, shivered pathetically in the wind. *A makeshift dwelling.*

The shock of this discovery brought with it a flurry of ambivalent emotions. I immediately felt a trespasser. I had crossed a private threshold. As moments passed I wondered at the circumstances that would drive an individual to seek habitation up here, in a derelict building exposed to the elements? What measure of courage, of tenacity, would be required to share this landscape with the wild voices of night, with the cold, the wind and the rain? But what gifts, also, would morning bring? Could I endure up here, I asked myself, if put to the test?

Looking around I noticed that parts of the building had been hastily rebuilt as a bulwark against the wind. These small measures, it seemed to me, born out of expediency and necessity, were more than anyone had done for any of these ruins in over a century. They constituted a restoration from *derelict* to *dwelling*. Heapey Moor farm had become – even if only for the briefest period – a home again. For all the gestures that I had made over the previous few years, these simple ones, made by an anonymous vagrant, were more restorative, more fitting and profound.

Reflecting on these events now, years later, I wonder if my wayward moorland path was heading in a similar direction? I think again of the etymology of the word. Anglez-arke. *Anlaf's erg*. A pasture with shepherd's hut or bothy – a temporary dwelling, long deserted. *Auðnar-hús*. A vacancy.

The muted language of the landscape. Was there a tacit invitation written in the lines of its hills, its streams and broken walls?

> Can you not feel it? Winter, calling each in, blithely
> gathering? Marking your place amongst us. Hill and bone.
> Skin and heather.

What if I were to submit to such a call? Perhaps I sensed something darker; an undertow, a pull, whose touch made me recoil. *The river and its promise*. It demanded too much, and I was not yet ready. My elaborate, self-sabotaging plans to bridge the distance between us through footfall could simply have been a plea for deferment, for respite.

During those months of irresolution, which I filled by compiling the text that later became the first edition of *Landings*, a chapter of my life slowly, gently, came to an end, and a new one opened. In due course I visited other landscapes, other countries. And yet the lure of Anglezarke remained. It spoke across vast distances. Through memory and maps, through books and documents in the public record.

Recently my writings have been scattered with Lancashire dialect quotations, with lexical remnants and traces from Gaelic, Icelandic and Anglo-Saxon. Where before I collected fragments found on my visits to the moor, I now gather words that were once used to call upon the landscape. Words that in many cases have long fallen out of use; folk-names, archaisms, forgotten idioms.

A pertinent example is *ark*, given its incidental connection with Anglezarke. Although not dead, the word seems to have become denuded – reserved now for use in a very specific, biblical context. But in previous centuries it had more life, particularly as part of a compound phrase:

> *Ark*, SB. a press to keep clothes in; a large chest for holding meal
> or flour. About Oldham and Hollinwood *ark* is a repository. The
> country 'badger' (q.v.) or provision-dealer will say *malt-ark, flour-*
> *ark, meal-ark*, and so on. A.S. *arc, earc*, a coffer, chest, vessel.

Compound words such as these remind me of the literary device known as *kenning*, a poetic trope found in Old Norse and Anglo-Saxon alliterative verse:

> Him se yldesta   ondswarode,
> werodes wīsa,   word-hord onlēac

Here the act of speaking is likened to unlocking a word-hoard, a metaphorical vessel for language. The sense of *ark* as an 'everyday store' is relevant here too. A vocabulary is a living language. Constantly in use. By contrast the word-ark that exists in the pages of old lexicons is a treasury. An ossuary. A box of relics.

Brog (N. Lanc.), SB. a branch, a bough, a broken branch.
Cf. W. *brigyn*, a top branch, a twig; *brigau*, the tops of trees.

But if language is constantly evolving, ever changing, why exhume
these remnants, these vestigial forms? Surely their usefulness
has long passed? Haven't they been superseded, made obsolete?
Perhaps there is a glimpse of something behind the words – a hint
at a way of looking at the world that is now also lost, an attention
to the form of things and a care, a generosity, in the bestowing of
names. *Brog* is not simply a branch, but a broken branch. *Lum*
is not just a pool, but a deep pool. And even where there are
synonyms in the contemporary lexicon, isn't there something to
be said for diversity, for fecundity? Each word has its own feel on
the tongue, its own sound, an inherent poetry. Moreover, each
word tells us something subtly different about its referent, and our
attitudes towards it.

Glisk, V. to glitter, shine, sparkle, glisten.
Low, SB. a flame. Icel. *log*, a flame.
Eawl-leet (pron. of *owl-light*), SB. twilight.
Shude, SB. the husk of grain, chaff.

Dictionaries and glossaries are vital in preserving these archaisms
for posterity, but despite the dignity conferred in being written
down, the words themselves are at risk of becoming little more
than curiosities. Quaint folkisms of a bygone era. *Ark*. A press
to keep clothes in. But what if I were to clothe myself in these
forgotten words? To incorporate them into fresh, living writing?
Could I lift them from behind the museum glass of old books?
Breathe life into them? Moreover, could these old forms vivify and
invigorate contemporary language, by virtue of their difference,
their strangeness?

CUSTODY

In recent months, a document came to my attention which cast
new light on the moor and its future. It made me remember that I
had, rather naïvely, called the moor a wilderness. Nothing could be
further from the truth. As part of the West Pennine Moors it has
been managed since the 1970s by a partnership that now comprises
seven local authorities, regional agencies, the water provider
United Utilities and several special interest groups, including
those representing wildlife conservancy, community interests and
recreational users. The document in question is a ten-year vision for
the area, published in 2010, which cites the European Landscape
Convention as a pivotal covenant that formally recognises
'landscapes as law', seeking to establish and implement policies
aimed at landscape protection, management and planning.

The document's scope is far too diverse and complex for me to
summarise here, but amongst the objectives outlined are those
to enhance biodiversity, reduce erosion and flooding, conserve
and restore moorland landscape (including blanket bog, fringe
woodland, grassland, meadow and pasture), control invasive
and non-native species, promote sustainable farming and land
management, implement a holistic approach to water catchment
and improve public access (whilst also minimising the impact
caused by tourism and recreation).

Buried amongst the plethora of lists and tables is the proposal to
'conserve and enhance key historic landscape features, particularly
those associated with the agricultural and industrial landscape. For
example: drystone walls, hedgerows, derelict farm buildings, mill
ponds and lodges'.

At some point during the recent past, ruins such as those that
I encountered on Anglezarke Moor have come to represent

'heritage', rather than the contaminative problems associated with human habitation. It seems that their dereliction has become a key to their salvation. It is also rather fitting to note that amongst the parties charged with their custodianship is United Utilities – a water company and successor to the Liverpool Corporation.

I think back to my early encounters with the shattered remnants of Old Rachel's farm, on the southern banks of the fledgling River Yarrow:

> And as I clamber over wood and stone, trying to trace its
> perimeter – to distinguish it from the moor which threatens
> to engulf it – I dislodge bits here and there, unintentionally
> becoming complicit in the process of decay. And how to stop the
> rot? How to salvage something from time's passage? How long
> before the map makers decide to erase this structure completely?
> Before it becomes a nameless ruin? And then a mere pile of
> stones. Mossed over. Forgotten. How long until they lift its name
> from their charts and from our collective memory?

In 2006 the European Landscape Convention was ratified by the UK, and the covenant became binding the following year. It's strange to think that, whilst I was obsessing over the fate of these ruined buildings, legislation was being put into place which might afford them some form of protection.

The West Pennine Moors Management Plan (2010-2020) features on its cover a photograph of Drinkwaters – a ruin on the lower slopes of Great Hill, on the northern borders of Anglezarke. Of all the views in the West Pennine Moors – hills and water, heather and bracken – this seems to me a poignant choice. It can't help but feel emblematic. *This is what we want to save.*

Should I take comfort, then, in such measures? The plan mentions 'creating a good working relationship with tourist boards in order to ensure promotion of WPM heritage'. In this context, what exactly does 'conserve and enhance' mean? How can derelict piles of masonry and timber be transformed into a visitor attraction? Perhaps there will be an audit? Another anonymous archivist might compile a book of records with the purpose of recommending which ruins are worth remembering, worth conserving, and which can be forgotten.

In the meantime, the thankless custodians of these ruins are not a committee, but a flock. At night they huddle behind broken walls, making their ovine dwellings amongst the tumbled stones, nourishing the plants which grow there with their excrement. Perhaps it is fitting that these once-proud dwellings should eke out the rest of their existence in this manner? The business of farming still goes on throughout the Pennines, and although many of the people have departed, these animals still remain. A marker for something. An oblique form of testimony.

I have heard
Strange voices in the evening wind; strange forms
Dimly discovered throng'd the twilight air.

ABYSS

I remember, in those first days, sitting on the high banks of the fledgling river. Staring out at the expanse of moor that seemed to stretch into infinity.

Aire leagte air saoghail dhorcha.

It seemed as if the earth
had tipped on its axis.
That the moor swung
teetering beneath me.
That if I didn't cling
to the grass banks,
I would fall
into an abyss.

DESERTED

Attend to me.
Field where vigils are held.
Grazier. Watcher.
Keeper of the valley.

Auðn, wilderness, desert.
Field parcels. Ploughshares.
Oxgangs of land.
A royal domain.

Auðnar-hús, auðnar-sel.
Observatory. House where
there is a corpse.
October 7th, 2007.

ANGLEZARKE

The name remained long after Anlaf. Long after his people
had disappeared. It became a refrain. A melody sung in endless
variation by each generation, century after century, over the course
of a millennium.

But did endurance, longevity, perpetuity, bestow a kind of truth?
Did it come, at last, to work its way into the moor, and the moor
into it?

×	○	×
an	glez	arke

Could I reconstruct the landscape from its stress pattern? From
the rhythm, the cadence, of its utterance? Could I transcribe its
syllabic, its phonemic, music into pure vibration?

æŋ	gəlz	ark

And what of its myriad permutations? Is there a clue within each
subtle voicing, which, when gathered together, provides a key with
which to sound the landscape?

Aneles   Anneles

Andeleves   Andles

Angelz   Angles   Anglez   Angliz

Anliz   Anlisz

Anlas   Anlaz   Anles   Anlez

Anlaghes   Anleyz

Alase

Anlase   Anlaues   Anlawes   Anlewes

(h)erg   (h)arghe

argh   arghe   aregh

arwe   arewe

earche

arch   ark   arke

aregth   arath   aragth

FAÇADE

From afar the moor is a façade.
A hanging of pale canopies:

> *calico*
> *muslin*
> *hemp*

Rough cloths of muted grey,
yellow, green, brown. And
the sky a grey sheet.

But turn the corner
of the high lane above
Moses Cocker's and
the façade vanishes.
Wind-blown to nothing.

And in its place the vast,
looming earth.

And the river's yarn.

PROXIMITY

> *Bentyn*, s. the touch, contact; the sense of the touch or
> feeling – though *ennaghtyn* is rather used in this sense,
> v. to touch, to belong to; to reach or join to.

In the absence of proximity I am drawn ever inward. To spacial
memory. Place cells. Cognitive maps.

I visit the moor's simulacrum, transposed and mapped in cellular
miniature. But this terrain is shifting. It reveals itself unbidden.
Offers brief glimpses. Strange knots of sensory and emotional
tissue.

> A hawthorn tree by a broken wall on Burnt Edge.
> A sheep skull lying in the long grass by Brown Hill.
> A wooden fence in the pale fields above Calf Hey.

These things are so real, so vivid, that they quicken the heart.
But if I concentrate – if I focus too intently – they dissipate. The
landscape is somehow veiled. Beyond reach. Its meadows are
swathed in fog. Its ground, treacherous.

> *Ashlins*, s. a spirit, ghost, apparition, glorious vision. *Eisht*
> *hee'm yn ashlins bannee e laue yesh*. Pargys Caillit.

> *Ashlish*, *aislys*, s. a vision, a dream, a divine revelation in a
> dream, s. a winding sheet, i.e. *aaish-leine* or *leine-vaaish*,
> a death shirt.

MINIATURE

The landscape is here in miniature.

Phials of soil. Brook water. Alluvium from the river.
Bark and fragments of bone, shrouded in muslin.
A small box of feathers. A trove of leaves and seeds.
Husks. Shells. Sheddings.

Each a vessel for memories.

This small pebble. *Godstone.*
Is between Hempshaws and Simms
on the path where the stonechat is calling.
December 23rd, 2007.

Ütic, ütic. Flint knap. A minute cacophony. Multiple tiny
reverberations. Colliding with the sound of my footsteps on the
rough ground. Chack. Scuff. Churr.

And as I touch this stone the bird is calling still.
Claghan-ny-gleiee. Remember us. Speak of us.

Arrange them on the map.

Place them according to where each was found.

So as not to forget.

TESTIMONIES

Listening to these many hours of recordings, I find that I'm increasingly drawn to the inert space that borders the music. The near silence between notes. The edge-song of the moor itself. And interspersed with the sounds of bowed strings and concertina drone are recordings of transit, of movement across the moor. The circuit between Old Rachel's, Hempshaws and Simms, crossing the river twice. The old drove road that runs from White Coppice up to the high plateau of Heapey Moor. The low ridge that connects Noon Hill, Winter Hill, Hordern Stoops and Great Hill.

These are documents of time spent, not tied to a place, but adrift within it, constantly roaming, never dwelling. They are records of footfall, the oblique narrative of grass, sedge and heather trodden underfoot. Of exertion, of breath, of endeavour.

Half a decade later, I find these muted, awkward testimonies more moving, more expressive, than any of my musical compositions. They remind me that I took an elliptical path through the moor's quiet places. Moreover, they remind me that there are other pathways of which there is no trace. Pathways that overarch the landscape. The flight of birds, of insects. Transits of the sun and moon. The earthbound trajectory of leaves, blown from trees in the autumn. Pollen grains in the spring. And most of all, there are the pathways of the river, with all its hidden tributaries, its countless runnels, its myriad subterranean passages.

What would a map of all these paths look like? Could such a map exist?

THE RIVER BENEATH

There is a river
beneath the Yarrow.
This *other* is a dark
cascade. A black
and ceaseless torrent.
It is the lure
which all rivers
follow. And a line
that you can
never cross.

FEATHER

And
      the moor
                  rests
on a kestrel's feather.

Brid – air-bride.

Thou thing that holds gravity.

I bore you on my shoulders. I carried you.

ROOT

A music hovers, gentle, over the valley.

Yarwe. Earwe. Yarewe.

The river is the root. The open string.
Old Rachel's a fourth. Simms a fifth.

And the path between them.
The most ancient of melodies.

the river is both hand and tongue

its testimony written voiced seen heard

LINE

What line did the river first write in the valley?
What sense, made over and over, now senseless?

Dissolved salts. Glacial memories.
Inklings of maternal violence
written in moraines,
in alluvium,
in pulverised rock.

(A syllabary, loosened
from grit and clay.)

What is the true note deep within the foss,
heard, straining, above the froth and laughter?

An ancient, unchanging music
that scores valleys,
intones, beckons,
ushers them
into existence.

ECHO

Bassagh, A. belonging to the palm of the hand; flattish, low.

Could the miniature landscape of my palm, with its myriad intersecting lines, channels and meridians, its shallow valley, mirror that of the moor?

> *The proximal crease of the River Yarrow.*
> *The thenar eminence from Noon Hill to Winter Hill.*
> *The distal crease of Green Withins Brook.*
> *The hypothenar eminence from Will Narr to Great Hill.*

Or could I mnemonise the landscape along the joints of my fingers? A Guidonian hand. Each knuckle, each phalanx, a node in the lattice. A place. A sonority.

And with each articulation, each voicing, what new pathways could I trace across the moor? What hitherto unthought-of connections?

> *The tips of my thumb and forefinger bridging the gulf between Bromiley Pastures and Hurst Hill.*

What visions, imaginings, remappings?

> *The intertwining of my first and second fingers rewriting the paths of Dean Brook and Cote Slack, as if they sprang from the same source.*

A topology of touch. Of feeling. Calling upon the landscape through memory and gesture.

ANGLEZARKE	A: 191.6,	B: 1019.0,	C: 3550,	D: 46
CHORLEY	A: 10.1,	B: 48.3,	C: 990,	D: 39
RIVINGTON	A: 275.0,	B: 1841.0,	C: 6280,	D: 61
YARROW	A: 65.0,	B: 839.2,	C: 2894,	D: 103

A	Area in acres
B	Contents in million gallons
C	Embankment length in feet
D	Greatest embankment depth in feet

It strikes me now that I spent much of my time, particularly in those first few years, skirting the threshold of Anglezarke. Keeping watch over its southern border, marked out by the path of the Yarrow. The wrythen river.

There I traced pathways through the fields above Stoops and Old Rachel's. Along the high, fenced banks below Coomb. Down the steep meadow that flanks Noon Hill Wood.

This side of the river is Rivington. *Rowinton*. The wicken moor. Writing more than a century ago, William Fergusson Irvine described it as follows:

> Rivington is an oasis in a desert of rapidly blackening country. The encircling flames of industry are fast licking up all the green and tender things of life, leaving only an arid waste of cinder heaps. The curves of the oak and beech have given way to the straight chimney-shaft, while the farmstead with its quaint gables has been levelled to find space for gaunt factory walls. But at the borders of Rivington all this is stayed. A city thirty miles away must have water free from taint, and so a wide tract of hillside is chosen, and an invisible barrier encircles it, through which no factory may penetrate.

For all its lyrical hyperbole, Irvine's commentary is important because he was writing at a pivotal moment in the history of the landscape – namely its acquisition as watershed land by the Liverpool Corporation. Nevertheless it is difficult to accept Irvine's charitable characterisation of its new owner as protector of the environment. Clearly he saw the inexorable expansion of industry – the chimney-shafts and factory walls – as modernity's chief menace, and welcomed the attentions of reservoir builders if it afforded respite to the 'green and tender things of life'.

At the turn of the 20th century the landscape of Rivington and Anglezarke was far from untouched – the area already had a sandstone quarry, a lead mine, a bleach works and a cotton mill. Perhaps Irvine viewed the compromise that the waterworks scheme offered as a chance for salvation? A few farms could be sacrificed in order to protect acres of countryside. Nevertheless, I still wonder what he would have thought of the landscape a mere ten years later, when many of those farms on the high moor had become vacant, and their 'quaint gables' left to crumble. Moreover, I wonder what he would have made of the attitudes of those that followed him, a century later? After the smog of Victorian England cleared, the relics of coal-and-steam-powered industry became enshrined in museums, and its architecture was given a second life in towns and cities as façades for luxury apartments.

The 21st-century perception of this landscape is aptly summed up in a document recently published by Lancashire County Council, which, whilst acknowledging the impact of these large-scale engineering projects, emphasises their aesthetic worth and heritage value:

> The appropriation of the land by the water undertakings and consequent depopulation had a significant landscape impact. The remains of these farms are still extant. The reservoirs represent important feats of engineering and constructions, such as feeder conduits, overflow cascades and slipways, embankments and tunnels, are of historical significance. Victorian detailing of the built features of the reservoirs, including gothic style valve towers and crenellated stone walls with decorative reliefs, are important pieces of architectural heritage. Similarly remnants

of construction workers' dwellings and places of worship are
important reminders of the massive human input involved in
their construction.

That these structures are impressive, compelling even, is
undeniable. I remember being repeatedly drawn to the Yarrow
Reservoir, which seemed to occupy a focal position in the
landscape, cradled between the moors of Anglezarke and
Rivington. Situated on its western embankment is a bye-wash – a
large, stone stairway which runs down under Knowsley Lane and
into the Anglezarke Reservoir below. As an emergency feature
it only comes into use during periods of heavy rain (when the
overflow from the reservoir spills down its stepped channel), but
to me it always seemed like a link in a chain. Something vital. And
so, whenever I visited there during dry months I felt a sense of
dislocation, of discordance.

On such occasions I would replay the sounds I'd recorded
previously at Old Rachel's farm, up on the high moor near the
river's birthplace. I would sit and listen to the music of those
open grasslands as it welled-up, accruing dense, clamouring
reverberations in the concrete and ashlar confines of the waste-
weir. In these moments it seemed to me that sound could be a
surrogate for water, that it could represent movement, fluidity
and life where there was none. In many ways I felt a connection
between those deserted buildings on the high moor and the vacant
geometry of this arid channel. There was a deep sense of negative
space. Each was a vessel for something that had been lost.

Years later, I wonder if I am alone in expressing sadness at the
ruin of those ancient dwellings. This has led me to search for
solidarity in the words of others. R.S. Thomas's 'Nant-yr-Eira'.

Ted Hughes's 'Widdop', 'Wadsworth Moor' and 'Shackleton Hill'. George Mackay Brown's 'Burnmouth'. Thomas, in particular, who spent many years as a priest in the Welsh valleys, was unflinching in his depiction of the physical and emotional hardships endured by those who worked on the land. After reading many of his unsentimental, often bleak, poems, I wonder if the experience in the north-west of England was very different?

What would the moorland landscape of Rivington and Anglezarke look like now, if the Yarrow Reservoir had never been built? Would more of the farms have endured, or would their decline have continued regardless? Perhaps the reservoir scheme offered salvation not only to the landscape, but to the people who lived within it? Maybe to some it even presented an opportunity? The chance to make a better life – an escape from the burden of tradition, from poverty and toil.

MERE

The reservoir is a mere dub in the river. The water
slacks, momentarily. Is skimmed for human consumption.
But
        it
               pushes
                      on-
                             wards,
                                      re-
                            doubling
                     as it joins
              the black water,
dubh glaisi, du glais,
a swift arrow to the sea.

BOND

As the instrument has partaken
of the landscape – its body
bequeathed to soil, and later
exhumed –
so, a bond is made.

A pairing of movements. Of gestures.

The second finger hovers over the third fret.
The swift downwards stroke of the bow.
Kill note.

The string stopped with a feather touch.
A piercing cry.

And on the moor's edge
the red-brown bird takes up again.
Bridges the air above the Yarrow.
Its hunger momentarily sated.

LOOM

Loom house.
The farther gateway.
A small close
planted with trees.

A corruption
of Helmshaws.
A stone in the
left-hand side.

Shallow.
Incision.
The stone walls
are set.

There was a hamlet.
A.F. 1741.

LITANY

River –

theaw'rt ith' clifts oth' rocks,
ith' huddin places oth' ftairs,
le' me yer thy veighce;
for sweet is thy veighce.

A murmur –

'twixt clack un chunner.

A litany of names.

Of those who lived and died
within its compass,
who left their mark on the landscape
or who were forgotten –
who passed by like ghofts.

Each, the same, made equal in death.

Monny watters connot quench love,
noather con th' floods dreawn it.

Abbot, Abbott, Abot, Abut, Acroyd, Adams, Adderley, Aier, Ainscough, Ainsley, Ainsworth, Aldred, Alexander, Alker, Anderson, Anderto, Anderton, Andrews, Anesworth, Answorth, Antwells, Archer, Arnold, Arrowsmith, Artcher, Ashcroft, Ashton, Ashworth, Asley, Asmough, Aspden, Aspen, Aspinal, Aspinall, Asspin, Asten, Astin, Asting, Astley, Aston, Atcherley, Atherton, Auker, Aulsebrook, Austin, Backsendean, Backsondean, Bain, Baine, Baines, Bainforth, Baitson, Bakerstaff, Ball, Ballshaw, Ballshe, Balshaw, Bamber, Bane, Baneford, Bank, Banks, Bannister, Barker, Barlow, Barnes, Barns, Baron, Barry, Barton, Bate, Bateson, Batson, Battersby, Battson, Baxendale, Baxendeel, Baxendell, Baxondayn, Baxondean, Baxondein, Baxsondean, Baxter, Bean, Beard, Beardsworth, Beat, Beatson, Beaver, Beddoes, Beddows, Beesley, Bell, Benison, Bennet, Bennett, Bennison, Bentley, Bently, Berrey, Berry, Bibby, Bickerstaff, Bickley, Biggs, Bilinge, Bilsborrow, Birch, Birchall, Bircher, Birkett, Black, Blackburn, Blackely, Blackhurst, Blackledge, Blackley, Blacklow, Blagburn, Blaikley, Blake, Blakeley, Bleakley, Bleakly, Blundell, Boardman, Bollough, Bolton, Bomford, Bond, Booth, Boowith, Bordman, Bouth, Bow, Bowling, Bradley, Bradly, Bradshaw, Bramely, Bramwell, Brentnall, Bridge, Brierley, Brindel, Brindle, Broadhurst, Brodgen, Bromaley, Bromely, Bromiley, Bromily, Brook, Brooks, Brounlow, Browenlow, Brown, Browne, Brownlo, Brownlow, Brumwell, Bryers, Buckley, Bulough, Buloughh, Burchal, Burn, Burney, Burns, Burrow, Burry, Burton, Bury, Busy, Butlar, Butler, Buttlear, Cadmon, Calderbank, Caldwell, Carlisle, Carrington, Carruthers, Caston, Caterwell, Cathrial, Catterel, Cattrell, Caunce, Cave, Cawley, Cayton, Cershaw, Chadwick, Chalender, Chalinder, Challender, Challinder, Challoner, Chamberlain, Chambers, Charleston, Charnly, Charnock, Chilton, Chroston, Clark, Clarke, Clarkson, Claton, Clayton, Clough, Coalson, Cockar, Cocker, Cockshot, Coderbonk, Coker,

Coleson, Colleson, Collier, Colson, Compton, Conce, Conlif,
Conlith, Cook, Cooper, Corbet, Corley, Corner, Cotton, Coulin,
Coullin, Coulling, Cowburn, Crankshaw, Crichlow, Critchley,
Croft, Croke, Crompton, Cromton, Cronshaw, Crook, Crooke,
Cross, Crosson, Crossons, Crosston, Croston, Crowder, Crowther,
Cuerden, Cundliff, Cundlth, Cunlif, Cunliff, Cunliffe, Cunlive,
Curren, Dalton, Danby, Dandy, Darbeshire, Darbishire,
Darbyshire, Davenport, Davies, Davis, Dawson, Dean, Deichfild,
Dent, Derbishire, Derbyshire, Deurs, Devenport, Dewhurst,
Dickenson, Dickerson, Dickeson, Dickingson, Dickinson,
Dickson, Diconson, Digles, Dike, Ditchfield, Dixon, Dod, Doten,
Doton, Dotten, Drinkwater, Driver, Duckworth, Dudley, Dunn,
Dunstall, Duten, Dutten, Dutton, Duxbesy, Duxbury, Dyche,
Dyke, Eastham, Eastom, Easton, Eatock, Eaton, Eccleston,
Eddisford, Eden, Edge, Edisford, Egerton, Eley, Elison, Ellison,
Ellsmoore, Entwisle, Entwistle, Euxton, Exton, Fairbrother,
Fairclough, Fairtcluf, Fairust, Farbrother, Farington, Farmer,
Farnoth, Farnworth, Farrance, Farrel, Farriman, Farrington,
Fasackerly, Fawkes, Fearnley, Fenney, Ferest, Fernly, Fielden,
Fielding, Finch, Finsh, Fisharkarly, Fisher, Fizsik, Fletcher, Foaster,
Ford, Forest, Foster, Fowden, Fowler, Fox, Foy, France, Frances,
Friar, Frier, Frith, Froggart, Garbut, Gardener, Gardiner, Garner,
Garstang, Gaskell, Gaskill, Gaunt, Gaxson, Gelly, Gerrard,
Gibson, Gildert, Gilford, Gill, Gillibrand, Gladden, Gledhill,
Glossop, Goley, Golly, Goodacre, Gorton, Goulding, Gratricks,
Gray, Green, Greenalch, Greenalgh, Greenhalch, Greenhalf,
Greenhalgh, Greenhough, Greenwood, Gregory, Greston,
Gretricks, Gretriks, Gretrixs, Grexson, Grey, Grime, Grimshaw,
Grimshe, Gromley, Groundy, Grunday, Grundy, Guest, Guffog,
Guy, Hampson, Haddock, Haigh, Hale, Hall, Hallawell, Hallisdal,
Halliwel, Halliwell, Halls, Hallsall, Halluel, Halsall, Halslome,
Halsworth, Hamar, Hambleton, Hamer, Hamor, Hampson,

Hancock, Hankey, Hanson, Hardi, Harding, Hardy, Hargreaves, Hargreves, Hargroves, Harker, Harper, Harrison, Harrode, Hart, Harte, Harter, Hartley, Harvey, Hash, Haslam, Haslame, Haslem, Haslom, Haslome, Haslsame, Hasslam, Haston, Hatch, Hatfield, Hatton, Hauworth, Hawarden, Hawkins, Haworth, Hayes, Hayhurst, Haykinson, Heald, Heamer, Heap, Heapes, Heard, Heart, Heaton, Heddock, Helton, Hendry, Hershe, Hesford, Hey, Heydock, Heyes, Heys, Hibbert, Hickinson, Hickman, High, Higham, Higher, Highfield, Highiam, Higingson, Higson, Hill, Hillkton, Hilson, Hilton, Hind, Hindle, Hindley, Hindly, Hinley, Hinly, Hitchen, Hitchin, Hitching, Hobrauough, Hobrook, Hodgkinson, Hodkinson, Hodson, Hoghton, Holand, Holcroft, Holden, Holdin, Holding, Holland, Hollon, Hollt, Holm, Holme, Holmes, Holms, Holsworth, Holt, Homs, Hood, Hooly, Hoomes, Hope, Hops, Horabin, Hormbeyshire, Hornbey, Hornby, Horobin, Horraben, Horrabin, Horriben, Horrobin, Horrocks, Horrox, Horsfield, Houeth, Hougeth, Hough, Houghton, Houlby, Houldbrough, Houlden, Houlm, Houlmes, Houlms, Hoult, Houltt, Howard, Howarth, Howcroft, Howlcroft, Howorth, Hudson, Hugh, Hughes, Humphreys, Hunter, Hurd, Hurst, Hutchinson, Hyghfield, Ingham, Ince, Ingam, Ingram, Isherwood, Jackman, Jackson, Jaxson, Jelle, Jelley, Jelly, Johnson, Jolley, Jolly, Jones, Joyly, Jubb, Kay, Keaton, Kellet, Kenyon, Kerfoot, Kerfott, Kerkam, Kershaw, Kersley, Key, Kirkby, Kirkham, Kirkland, Knoles, Laithwaite, Lambert, Langdale, Lansdale, Latewith, Latham, Lathom, Lawton, Lea, Leach, Leadbetter, Leaming, Leaster, Leathwit, Ledger, Lee, Leech, Leeming, Leigh, Leister, Letus, Ley, Leyland, Liddel, Lifsley, Ligh, Lily, Lindley, Lingard, Lissaman, Little, Livesay, Livesie, Livesley, Livesy, Lomax, Longton, Longworth, Lonsdale, Loo, Lord, Lou, Low, Lowe, Lowton, Loyd, Lyon, MacDonald, Madcalf, Madder, Magnall, Makin, Making, Makingson, Makinson, Mangnal,

Mangnall, Mann, March, Markland, Marres, Marsden, Marsdin,
Marsh, Marshall, Marshell, Marſtin, Martelive, Marterland,
Martin, Mason, Massey, Mathar, Mather, Mathew, Matthews,
Maudesley, Maudsley, Mawdsley, Mayall, Mayhall, Maynal,
Maynall, Mayoh, Mayola, Mayor, McClane, McDonald,
McGuire, Meadows, Medcalf, Metcalf, Metcalfe, Middleton,
Miler, Millar, Miller, Mills, Milner, Minton, Mitchell, Molenex,
Molenux, Molineux, Mollineux, Mollyneux, Molyneux, Monk,
Monks, Moore, Morres, Morris, Morson, Mort, Moss, Moulden,
Mulenex, Mullineux, Murphy, Nab, Nailor, Narcross, Naylor,
Nelson, Newton, Nicholson, Nichonson, Nickinson, Nickison,
Nighgale, Nightengale, Nightgale, Nightingal, Nightingale,
Nightingall, Nihill, Nitingale, Nixon, Norcroft, Norcross, Norris,
Nowell, Nuttall, Nutter, Ogden, Ogdin, Ollerton, Ormbishire,
Ormesher, Orrabin, Orret, Orrit, Palmer, Park, Parkington,
Parkinson, Parr, Partington, Pass, Pearson, Pendlebury,
Penlington, Perpoint, Person, Petty, Philipson, Pickoup, Pickup,
Pierpoint, Pilkington, Pillkinton, Pimbley, Pimbly, Pimlet,
Pimley, Pinnington, Pitfield, Plowright, Pomfret, Porter, Potter,
Poumfret, Povey, Prescot, Prescut, Preſton, Proctor, Radcliff,
Radcliffe, Rainforth, Raneforth, Ratclif, Ratcliffe, Ratcliff,
Ratcliffe, Ratlif, Ratliff, Ratliffe, Ratlive, Rawlinson, Rawlison,
Rawſthorne, Read, Reancher, Reaſt, Reed, Rencher, Renshaw,
Reynolds, Richmon, Richmond, Rickman, Riding, Rigby, Rigg,
Riggot, Riley, Rimmer, Rivington, Roberts, Robinson, Rod, Roe,
Roper, Roscall, Roscoe, Roscough, Roscow, Rose, Roskow, Ross,
Rossburn, Rossow, Roſthern, Roſthorn, Roſtorn, Rothwell, Row,
Rowhill, Rowhlyson, Rutter, Sale, Sales, Salisbury, Salsburry,
Salsbury, Salt, Scarebrick, Scarnal, Scarnel, Scarnell, Scarsbrick,
Schofield, Scocroft, Scofield, Scot, Scotson, Scott, Scowcroft,
Seaton, Sedden, Seddon, Seed, Seenick, Sefton, Selby, Senior,
Settle, Sharpels, Sharples, Sharpls, Sharrock, Shaw, Shawe,

Shepherd, Sheppard, Sherburn, Sherrington, Sherwood, Sibrin, Siddal, Sim, Simm, Simme, Simms, Simon, Simpson, Singleton, Skoulcroft, Slater, Slaytor, Smalley, Smeathals, Smethills, Smethurst, Smith, Smithells, Smithels, Smithills, Smithson, Snape, Southworth, Spake, Speake, Speakeman, Spiby, Spurr, Standforth, Standforths, Standish, Stanley, Stephenson, Stevenson, Steveson, Steward, Stewart, Stirrup, Stones, Strange, Stuart, Stuarte, Stubbs, Sumner, Sunter, Sutcliffe, Sutton, Swabey, Sweet, Sweetlove, Swift, Swithenbay, Symm, Symme, Talar, Talor, Tar, Tatlow, Tattersal, Tattersall, Tatterson, Taylar, Tayler, Taylor, Tayor, Tebay, Teler, Teller, Temperton, Thelon, Thirkell, Thomason, Thompson, Thorburn, Thornley, Thornleys, Thornly, Thorp, Thorpe, Throp, Timperly, Tomasson, Tompson, Tomson, Tonge, Tongue, Tootel, Tootell, Tootle, Topping, Towler, Trelford, Tumpson, Tunstall, Turner, Tyrer, Tyrone, Unsworth, Valentine, Vallentine, Varden, Vauce, Vause, Veneson, Venison, Vennison, Voce, Voose, Waddicar, Waddicor, Waddicre, Waddiker, Waddilove, Waddington, Wadilove, Wadington, Wadinton, Wairing, Walch, Walden, Waley, Walkden, Walker, Walles, Walley, Walls, Walmsley, Walsh, Waltch, Walton, Walydon, Warburton, Warbutton, Ward, Warden, Wareing, Warmby, Warterworth, Water, Waters, Waterworth, Watmough, Watmouth, Watson, Weaters, Weaver, Webster, Welch, Wells, Wellsby, Welsby, Welsh, West, Westby, Whale, Whales, Whaley, Whalley, Whalls, Whally, Whaly, Whitaker, Whiteaker, Whitehead, Whitel, Whitelaw, Whiteside, Whitle, Whittaker, Whittle, Whole, Whom, Wil, Wilcock, Wild, Wilding, Wilgarden, Wilkinson, Willcock, Williams, Williamson, Willson, Wilson, Winstanley, Winstanly, Wood, Woodcock, Woodfild, Woods, Woodward, Woodworth, Woolsoncroft, Worsley, Worthington, Wrencher, Wrenshaw, Wriding, Wright, Yate, Yates, Yearnshaw, Yeate, Yeates.

I have laid me down
Beside yon valley stream, that up the ascent
Scarce sends the sound of waters now, and watch'd
The beck roll glittering in the noon-tide sun,
And listened to its ceaseless murmuring.

WORD-HOARD

2 0 1 5

It has been nearly half a decade since I formally added to *Landings*.
Much of the work that formed the last adjunct, *Names. Dates.
Genealogies.*, was written in absentia, whilst living on the west
coast of Ireland. It reads to me now like an attempt to construct
a simulacrum – in the absence of the land itself I turned to the
many artefacts gathered from my years on the moor, 'each a
vessel for memories'. With the pressing distance of both time and
geography I felt compelled to 'Arrange them on the map. Place
them according to where each was found. So as not to forget.' A
small stone, for example, recalled a stonechat's voice amongst the
furze on December 23rd, 2007, and I had written Westell's phrase,
'ütic, ütic', in my notebook. From stonechat to stone, I had picked
up the pebble and added 'Remember us. Speak of us.' *Bird. Stone.
Place. Language. Memory.* All conflated.

If even such a seemingly meagre event is significant – receiving
its own artefact, its *thing-poem* – how to come to terms with the
sheer volume of experience, the clamour of voices? The archive
that *is* Anglezarke has an unspeakably complex order of inter-
relations – its index is constantly being extended and recompiled.
Each object is a nexus for multiple experiences, lives, energies –
both consecutively and simultaneously. The land is in continual
flux, from hay meadow to moor, valley to reservoir, hill-side to
plantation. Buildings reconfigure themselves as walls, bridges and
feeder conduits, or else they are assimilated into the bloated body
of the moor itself, whose very name shifts over the centuries –
Andelevesarewe, Anlauesargh, Anlewesearche. There is no rest.

When faced with the scale of such a task, the mind attempts to
distill, to rarefy, to simplify. The archivist becomes one of Meikle's
threshing contraptions, trying to separate the wheat from the
chaff. But it is useless, and by the end the endeavour has devolved

into list-making. *Names. Dates. Genealogies.* ends with a litany – a roll-call of names salvaged from parish and census records, 'each the same made equal in death'. In naming we can at least acknowledge or bear witness, and amongst the throng I see familial names, connections, footholds, but in the deluge I cannot quite hold on, and I fall. The many pages of appendices that follow – list after list, arranged and ordered into columns, cross-referenced, footnoted and summarised, are a futile – almost absurd – attempt to recover as much as possible, and the act of compiling becomes a kind of compulsion; the word-hoard an end in itself.

In this context, the printed page is therefore at best an interim report, an increment, a summary – obsolete before the ink has dried. There is always more to add, and, like the stonework of Anglezarke, its materials are endlessly reused. Over the subsequent years there are addenda: *Moor Glisk*, a book which uses *Landings* as its source, amongst other texts, to retell the landscape history of the county of Lancashire during the Industrial Revolution. The grids and columns of *Landings* have now disappeared as the text is scattered across the page, imitative of the violence of the period:

tracts of land   riven

apart

ploughing
burning
sowing
harrowing

milk produced from burning timber

the forest yields   at daybreak

47,000 acres

the sky
harnessed

ſpun

Limnology follows shortly thereafter, and its words are hurled
with even more violence, this time suggeſtive of riverine processes,
cascading down the book's valley and into its crevices and recesses.
The archiviſt's mentality is again in evidence as a glossary of over
1,000 water-words forms the book's appendix, gathered from
the new landscape in which I found myself – the Furness hills
of Cumbria – and from tributaries in the Celtic and Germanic
languages.

In the years that follow, my wife Autumn and I begin to formulate
answers to the queſtions of this new environment. Under her
influence the survey broadens to incorporate not juſt the human
catalogue of loss, but that of the native flora and fauna – a
deſtruction often brought about by human endeavour. Our work
begins to centre upon Ulpha Fell, a toponym that alludes to the
presence of wolves. We read and discover a country-wide hiſtory of
persecution and extirpation. Further research uncovers a ſtartling
fact – that all but the higheſt fells were once covered with trees.
Deep beneath tarns such as Devoke Water are pollen drifts, relics
of the great wildwood – a wilderness of the Mesolithic. What
remains today is in effect a waſteland – the result of suſtained and
wideſpread deforeſtation. Without the trees' roots to secure the
soil, and their deadfall to replenish it, centuries of precipitation
and weathering have denuded the landscape, leaving exposed
outcrops, crags and scars.

A new tension enters our work, with the list-poem at its heart, at once an invocation and celebration of what is here, and also an elegy for what has disappeared. This conflict between presence and absence, present and past, is epitomised by two new works: *A List of Probable Flora* and *Relics*. The former is a roll-call of plants of the high fells, many of them grasses – things trodden underfoot, ignored, forgotten. The latter is a calling-back to the oldest known names of the trees that once populated the uplands around Devoke Water – names such as *aikô (oak), *bherəg- (birch) and *salik- (sallow).

In the context of epochs, of glaciation and interglacation, of the slow transformation of a landscape and its ecosystems, the plight of a few isolated farmsteads, as depicted in *Landings*, begins to look small. Moreover, it becomes clear that farming itself has significantly contributed to this environmental degradation. The transition from a nomadic, hunter-gatherer mode of living to a settled, agrarian one involved the clearing of trees, the domestication of animals, the cultivation of plants and the extermination of predators – in short, the wholesale modification of the land. Where once I had seen the moor as a menacing presence that threatened to engulf the remnants of human existence, I now began to see humanity itself as a threat to the land, a disturber of its delicate ecology.

QUIET FURY

Looking back to *Landings*, I see these issues being debated on
a personal scale – the 'forgetful earth' weighed against my own
'intrusions into its sanctified chambers'. The regenerative processes
of the soil which erase my footprints and deny my memory is
therefore 'hideous', but there is also a sense of guilt that I make
an impression at all, and a desire for reciprocity, to 'bear its scars'
in return for my own. This longing for a physical union, 'to find
my place amongst' the stones and grasses is tempered by a kind
of chaste repulsion, and the relationship remains unresolved,
hovering on the edge of consummation.

Such ambivalence is reflected in the *other* testimonies that scatter
throughout the book: there are both entreaties and rebukes,
questions and answers – but to whom does each voice belong?
Like the litter trail of place-names they become untethered,
disembodied, indistinct – gathering here and there as echoes,
resonances, melodies – a 'residual undersong' that suffuses the
very landscape. This enmeshing of the self and non-self, human
and non-human, is a kind of anthropomorphism. At its root is an
empathic horror for the unvoiced and the unnamed, and a desire
to seek redress – but in becoming a receiver and translator do I
not risk instead putting words in their mouths, ascribing my own
thoughts and feelings, externalising the internal? The answer is,
of course, yes, but in *Landings* the risk is worth it, because the
alternative is a great silence, a disconnect, an exile from the world
itself.

Some archaeologists have theorised that the human empathic
ability evolved structurally within the Upper Palaeolithic brain,
enabling hunters to identify with their quarry and therefore
better predict animal movements. To the sensitive mind it seems
something of a tragedy that the faculty which connects us to other

animals is also an instrument for their entrapment, but we might also remember that love is often depicted as a form of wounding – that Eros himself carried a bow and arrow. From European pre-history there are carvings, inscriptions and artefacts that allude to an antlered or horned god, indicating that the divine and the animal were perceived as inherently connected. It is quite possible that no small reverence was reserved for the subject of the hunt, and that to partake of an animal's flesh was also to partake of the deity which it embodied – that, apart from its life-sustaining properties, it was also thought to transmit something of the animal's vital essence – its strength, agility and fertility. In the Christian epoch we can see an echo of that complex yoking of love, reverence and death in the Eucharist meal, in which Christ's body, later pierced by the Spear of Longinus, offers to those who consume it that ultimate godly essence – eternal life.

RELIQUARY

In an earlier edition of *Landings*, since revised, I questioned whether the girl-ghost, SP, would want to be remembered: 'Is there release in oblivion?' I asked, 'Are things under the soil best left there?' The desire to acknowledge and record the passing of things, both deeply personal and also peripheral, can't help but involve a risk of transgression. Do I have the right to speak for the others that I encounter, both human and non-human? Memory is a form of resistance, and there is a concomitant pull towards surrender, towards forgetting, just as sound recedes into silence. Selfhood brings with it a kind of awful awakening; a dawning sense of separation, of being alone. If the *other* is everything that is not us, how can we hope to know it, and by knowing, speak of it? When we reach out with language, do we hear anything but our own echo? Here in Cumbria, whilst walking in the Furness hills, I find that I am often searching for those rare moments of inner quiet where language ends and thought recedes. It is only then that I feel a sense of presence – a dissolving of the boundaries of the self and a connection to that which is beyond. But if this sense is a supra-lingual faculty, how then can we meet it with language?

Whilst researching *Moor Glisk* I came across the following commentary by Eilert Ekwall, referencing Lancashire toponyms: 'very few names testify to a feeling for natural beauty'. It reminded me that I had once written about the 'inherent poetry' of the Lancashire dialect – of the worth of words beyond mere utility. *Glisk* itself is one of the few words I uncovered in Nodal & Milner's glossary that seems to revel in beauty. It means 'to glitter, shine, sparkle, glisten'. Another associated term is *glizzen*, 'to sparkle'. Most of the remaining words in the book are grounded in things, they are functional, and perhaps reflect a certain kind of material reality.

In the preface to *Names. Dates. Genealogies.* I wrote about the
mediating effects of being a visitor to Anglezarke. In recent years
Autumn and I have sought to live within the landscapes that
are the focus of our work. In Ireland we rented a cottage in the
Burren, and both *Verse of Birds* and *The Flowering Rock* arose out
of the patch of land surrounding us. When settling in Cumbria,
we rented a cottage on a working farm in a remote valley in the
Dunnerdale Fells. Over the subsequent years we have intimately
experienced the complex rhythms of rural life, and have witnessed
first-hand the difficulty with which the upland landscape is
farmed. The soil, rendered poor by centuries of human endeavour
and attritional weather, is considered fit only for grazing sheep – a
self-perpetuating cycle which necessitates both the use of fertilisers
for the land and food supplements for the livestock. It is a hard
life, and it breeds a certain stoical, if not belligerent, temperament.

There is therefore a singular kind of economy which pervades
much of rural life – everything has a purpose, is used, reused
and often transformed – bent to new ends. A farmer I know
has a pile of scrap metal in his yard, constantly plundered for
running repairs. Farm machinery is scrupulously cleaned – not
out of a sense of pride, but to maximise the working life of every
component before it too becomes part of the scrap pile. I can't
help but feel that this economy extends also to language – that the
beauty of words is incidental to their function, their usefulness.
Shortly after arriving here I heard a farmer use the word *gersins*,
pointing to a plot of upland pasture – a word straight out of Nodal
& Milner's 1875 glossary. I was unspeakably moved that such a
word had endured into the 21st century, but of course the truth
was that it simply still had currency. Why throw something out
when it could be put to good use?

There are other words in the glossary that speak beyond utility. Interestingly, many of these relate to plants:

> *Corn-boggart*, SB. a scare-crow.
>
> *Jinny-green-teeth*, SB. literally the green scum on ponds, but supposed to imply the presence of a water-sprite or 'boggart'; a terror to children as they pass the pond on which the appearance is seen.
>
> *Ragged-robin*, SB. the meadow-lychnis (*Lychnis flos-cuculi*).
>
> *Robin-run-i'-th-hedge*, SB. the plant bedstraw (*Gallium*).

Folk-names such as these endured beyond Linnaeus, even into the modern age, and contain within them a dim echo of an ancient music that harmonised the human and the natural, a music that sang the names of a thousand nature spirits, names such as Ēostre, the Green Man, Herne, Hob, Jack-by-the-Hedge, John Barleycorn, the May Queen, Peg, Puck and Robin Goodfellow. Belief in the existence of such spirits began to diminish with the coming of Christianity, and the transition from polytheism to monotheism. By the time of Nodal & Milner, the idea of a sentient landscape was condemned as superstition, but it is interesting to speculate as to whether old beliefs continued to be held in the more isolated hills and valleys.

The question we must therefore ask is how representative such glossaries can be, and what methodological issues compromise their accuracy and completeness? Nodal & Milner's book seems to have been largely compiled from secondary sources – from the previously published glossaries, monographs and word-lists of highly literate writers, doctors and members of the clergy. We might therefore ask – what was the relationship between these professionals and the working populace that they sought to

represent? How could they hope to record the breadth of public
and private language, and the idioms of a way of life that was not
their own? What questions were asked and what, if anything, was
held back by those who were questioned?

Throughout *Landings* I returned again and again to the empty
space at the edges of maps, to the blank pages in the public record
– 'What name did this place have before records began?' I asked,
'What happened to the polyonymy of place?' There is a sense, in
this obsession with archives, lists and records, that I was searching
for something that can never be found, because it was never
recorded. Words spoken and lost to the morning air, muttered to
the fire as it sparked into life, whispered to the animal in the fold.
Or perhaps those words were never spoken, but were kept unsaid,
held in the mouth, conserved, protected? Or, indeed, there might
have been an intuitive understanding that such moments are
beyond language – that thought and intellect take us out of that
very presence – that connective tissue – which is the innate gift of
all things.

CHEMICAL

MEMORIES

2019

LIMBS

find the lost shieling
in earthen voices

see the valley edging its days
towards night

and what is left?
overflow of the book

hold back its sea-sick torrent
if you can

dredge the waters
for the limbs of feelings

BEGINNINGS

In 2005 I wrote the following about the difficulties of beginnings:

> How to begin writing this down? ... If I were to say – a robin
> sings in the trees across the field from this coppice – would that
> be enough? Could you flesh things out from such a meagre
> outline?

But despite these shortcoming, I later asked:

> ... could any film, recording or photograph tell you this? That
> whilst I dwelt within that wooded chamber, listening to those brief
> glimmers of song, I forgot about her, the river and its promise.

Words, for all their failings, speak. Or rather their voices are heard
where other forms of communication are mute. As sounds recede
into silence the written or printed word seems more enduring.
Even the apparently lost can be found, reclaimed, and written
again. *Yarwe. Earwe. Yarewe.*

But sounds, too, might also endure:

> Is there ever 'eventual silence'? When sounds recede below
> the threshold of hearing, perhaps they linger, nevertheless.
> Diminishing but never gone completely. Commingling with
> the residual undersong – the map and vessel of all melodies.

This idea of an *undersong* – unheard but intuited – has informed
many of my musical endeavours over the past decade. What would
it be like if I could amplify those residual sounds? Could I become
a string, resonating in sympathy with the landscape's inaudible
melodies?

And, of course, images speak too. In other ways.

Over the half decade or more that I visited the West Pennine Moors I made countless Polaroid images. The 'instant' nature of this medium was ideally suited to my purpose. The photograph could be left in situ, shortly after the moment of its creation.

> I want to make some kind of gesture. An offering. A mark of passing. And to leave it here. Tied to the land.

Some of these images I kept, however. Mementos, possibly. Perhaps I couldn't bear to leave everything behind. All these years later, I try to recollect the reasons why I didn't publish them along with the writings and music. Was it because I wanted to hold something back, to keep something private, and therefore secret?

Revisiting these images now I see that they are largely failures in the conventional photographic sense. They are over- or under-exposed, blurred, out-of-focus, or spoiled during the peel-apart process. Perhaps, like my progress along the many hidden tracks across the moor, I was unsure of foot, and turned back.

But it is precisely their uncertain status that lends these images their special quality, their supra-lingual power to evoke.

During that first visit to the copse at the brow of Sheep House Lane I made a number of Polaroids, one of which I kept. It spoke loudly, but its language was hermetic. Looking at it now, I might just as well try to transcribe the song of the robin from memory. Here is a meagre outline:

Twilight. The copse's dark mass, and against it, five individual trees standing out in paler colours. The two in the foreground are almost luminous. All five appear to shift, to twist. *Wriðan*, to writhe. On closer inspection they appear to fade in and out – only partially existing within the world of the picture, and partially somewhere else.

> *Blash*, SB. a sudden flame.
> *Gliff*, SB. a glimpse, a transient sight.

This effect is, of course, motion-blur – an artefact of a slow shutter-speed and an unsteady hand. It goes some way towards explaining the picture, but it does nothing to quieten it.

In 2010, writing in absentia, I noticed that my memory of Anglezarke was fleeting, insubstantial:

> The landscape is somehow veiled. Beyond reach. Its meadows are swathed in fog. Its ground, treacherous.

Looking at this image nearly a decade and a half after it was made, it gives me the same sensation of being unmoored. Cast adrift. The terrain is shifting, it is somehow *other*.

You must forgive me if I refrain from sharing the Polaroid here. It would appear, after all, that some things must be held back. As with those other photographs that appear in *Landings*, this one will exist as a ghost presence. Hovering on a threshold.

And so again I return to the facility of language to speak. I must make further appeals to your imagination. You must flesh things out from here.

VISION

and this vision
from the margins
of history

the photograph
draining the dusk
from trees

the map
holding the heads of fields
under water

GIRL-GHOST

Recently, I returned again to the photograph of Old Rachel's farm and the Evans family, made nearly half a century before the anonymous author of *the book* came to record their absence, and the farm's subsequent ruin. Unfortunately Lancashire County Council, who own the archive to which the image belongs, could offer no information on who originally made it, or the purpose behind this rather formal documentation of rural life. They could, however, offer a 'new' version of the image, which, magically, reveals two new figures in its composition.

This new print confirms that my original was cropped, as in the far right of the frame there now appears the head of a very young boy, side on, formally dressed and wearing a hat, his torso obscured by the bank wall.

The second figure, obscured by shadows in the original, stands in the doorway behind the 'woman in white'. She is dressed in dark clothes, wears a hat and has her hands clasped to her chest. It is remarkable to see her emerge from darkness. Are her crossed hands an act of modesty, of reticence, or does she offer up a prayer, or even join them together in suppressed delight at this rare, and presumably prestigious, event?

Sadly, this new image does nothing to shed any further light on the girl who 'crouches beneath the window cradling an infant, almost receding into the wall itself'. She is still an enigma.

The cover for this edition of *Landings* features a photograph of an anonymous 'little spinner' in the Globe cotton mill, Augusta, Georgia, USA. Before finding her, I looked for a photograph of a farm or mill worker from Lancashire, but could find nothing that resonated in quite the same way as this compelling image.

In the early 20th century, the photographer Lewis Wickes Hine
was employed by the National Child Labor Committee to
document examples of children who were put to work in mills
and factories across America. Hine made notes about each subject.
About one boy, who wasn't sure of his age, but thought that he was
perhaps 14 years old, Hine wrote 'Didn't look it. Has worked more
nights than day time.' About the nameless spinner girl he simply
wrote 'the overseer admitted she was regularly employed.'

The brevity of Hine's notes remind me of the anonymous author
of *the book*.

> What emotions linger at the edges of those pages?
> What words unsaid?

I think again of Ralph Marsden from Wilkinson Bullough, a farm
that overlooked the Yarrow valley before it was flooded. On the
1841 census he is listed as a 'weaver' at seven years old. Or else I
think of Alice Holt, a 'winder', at the age of ten.

And, of course, I think of SP. Farm serving girl in 1881. Buried in
1887, a young woman. The web of her life finished.

> *Deawnt*, v. finished; taken off or taken down. *Deawin'*, finishing,
> PT. Lancashire weavers call the web, or piece of cloth they are
> working upon, whether woollen or cotton, a 'cut'; and when the
> entire piece of web is woven, and taken off the loom, the weaver
> says he has 'deawnt his cut'; that is, he has taken his finished web
> down from the loom. So, figuratively, a man who dies has finished
> the web of his life.

THE PHOTOGRAPH

she looks downwards
as if expressing
her reticence

her objection
her complicity
her twilight

as if exposing her greenness
her doublings
her dark feathers

as if she sees
the black course of the river
its ruin and its divinity

THE WEAVER'S BURDEN

a woman steps out
of a century of shadows

a bird holds the sky's lease
a river's ends are tied

meanings warp
at the thread edge

of the canal

why cannot
the eye

see through
its weave

hanks of yarn
drawn together

the archive lies

COMPASS

where

to

find

the   unnamed   on   the   compass

of

the

lost

BECOMING

and the moor
is becoming
itself at last

archivist
turn your
heavy-bodied
night-flying
eyes away

the document
must remain
untitled

APPENDICES

LANCASHIRE

DIALECT TERMS

Transcribed from
A GLOSSARY OF THE LANCASHIRE DIALECT
BY JOHN H. NODAL & GEORGE MILNER, 1875

- *Boother, Boother-stone*, SB. (var. pron.) a boulder-stone.
- *Borrans* (N. Lanc.), SB. rough, craggy places, to which foxes run for safety. Gael. *borr, borra*, a knob; *borrach*, a projecting bank.
- *Brant*, ADJ. steep, as applied to a hill. Thus Brant Fell, near Windermere; Brantwood, Coniston, a wood on a steep hill side. Sw. *brant*, steep; Icel. *brattr*, steep. Cf. W. *bryn*, a hill.
- *Breast-hee*, SB. the mouth of a tunnel leading to a coal-pit which has been made in the side of a hill, the shaft being horizontal instead of vertical.
- *Bunhedge*, SB. a hedge made of twisted sticks.
- *Bury-hole*, SB. a grave: a word generally used by children.
- *Carr*, SB. a marshy place; a flat, low-lying land. Dan. *kær*, a marshy place. Cf. Sc. *carse*. There is a place called Gatley Carrs a few miles south of Manchester.
- *Carrwater*, SB. red peaty water.
- *Carry*, ADJ. red, peaty.
- *Carry-pleck*, SB. a place boggy with carrwater. Cf. A.S. *plæc*, a space.
- *Ceckly* (Mid. E. and S. Lanc.), *Cockly* (N. Lanc.), ADJ. unsteady, uneven.
- *Clag* (N. and E. Lanc.), V. to adhere. A.S. *clæg*, sticky earth, clay; Dan. *klæg, kleg*, loamy, sticky.
- *Claw* (Fylde), *Cleaw* (S. and E. Lanc.), *Cloose* (N. Lanc.), *Clow* (E. and Mid. Lanc.), SB. a floodgate in a watercourse. From Lat. *claudere*.
- *Clod*, SB. the ground. Cf. Dan. *klat*, a bit of ground.
- *Cloof*, SB. a clough, a wooded ravine. Icel. *klofi*, a cleft or rift in a hill closed at the upper end. Mid. E. *clough*.
- *Coppy*, SB. a small field.
- *Crow-gate*, SB. the direct road, as the crow flies.
- *Cut*, SB. a canal.

- *Dag*, SB. dew on the grass. Icel. *dögg*, dew; see also Icel. *deigr*, damp, wet, lit. 'doughy'. Cf. Icel. *deig*, dough; Mœso-Goth. *daigs*, dough, from a verb of which the earliest trace is the Mœso-Goth. *deigan*, to form by hand, as a potter forms clay.
- *Dag*, SB. to trail in the dew, wet, or mire. Icel. *döggva*, to bedew.
- *Dale* (Chipping; and Burrow, near Kirkby-Lonsdale), SB. an unseparated portion of a field, belonging to a second owner, and which is often unmarked, or only shown by stakes in the hedge and stones at the corners of the dale. A.S. *dæl*, a portion.
- *Dene, Deyn* or *Deign* (E. Lanc.), SB. a little valley. A.S. *denu*, a valley.
- *Dub*, SB. a pool, a marshy place, a muddy hole. Probably of Celtic origin; Cf. Irish *dób*, a gutter; W. *dwfr*, water.
- *Dummock*, SB. a small heap of soil or dirt. Prob. a dimin. of *dam*. Cf. Du. *dam*, a bank; Icel. *dammr*.
- *Eä* (N. and E. Lanc.), SB. a river or the channel of a river; applied also to water generally. A.S. *eá*, water. Mœso-Goth. *ahwa*. Icel. *á*. The word *eá* occurs four times in the A.S. version of Genesis II. 11-14, where the authorised version has river.
- *Flash-pit*, SB. a pit nearly grown up with reeds and grass.
- *Flosh* (Furness), SB. water, or a watery place.
- *Force* (N. Lanc.), SB. a cascade or waterfall. A fall of water in a narrow gorge. Icel. *fors*; Dan. *fos*.
- *Frith* (N. Lanc.), SB. a wood; also unused pasture land. W. *ffrith*.
- *Fub* (Ormskirk), SB. long withered grass on old pastures or meadows.
- *Gank*, SB. a deep, narrow footway.
- *Gate*, SB. a road, a way; also a manner or fashion; speed, rate

of movement. Icel. *gata*, A.S. *geat*, a way.

- *Goit, goyt*, SB. a watercourse to a mill.
- *Hag* (N. Lanc.), SB. an enclosure, a wood. A.S. *haga*, what is hedged in, a garden, a field; Icel. *hagi*, a hedged field.
- *Hare-gate*, SB. an opening in a hedge, sufficient for the passage of hares.
- *Headbolt* (Ormskirk), SB. a road over a bog or morass, stopped at one end.
- *Hippings, hipping-stones*, SB. pl. stepping-stones in a brook. Bungerley Hipping-stones, across the Ribble, near Clitheroe, so called to this day, are mentioned in Warkworth's Chronicle, A.D. 1470, where the word is spelt 'hyppyngstones'. Hipping is a form of hopping: 'That hippe aboute in Engelonde' (*Piers Plowman*, B, XV. 557).
- *Hoyt*, SB. a long road.
- *Intack*, SB. an enclosed piece of common. Cf. Icel. *ítak*.
- *Knowe*, SB. pronun. of knoll.
- *Leawk, leawks*, SB. pl. tufts of barren dry grass; locks of hair.
- *Leech*, SB. a pond or pool of water; water lying in the hollow of a road. In old Lancashire deeds and inquisitions the word appears frequently as *lache*, as in Blake-lache, Brad-lache, Grenelow-lache, Gos-lache and Mesdhaw-lache, always indicative of a marshy locality.
- *Ley*, SB. pasture or grass land, as distinguished from plough land or such as is kept under tillage.
- *Loane*, SB. a lane. A.S. *láne*, lone.
- *Lum*, SB. a deep pool.
- *Manigate* (Ormskirk), SB. a straight road over bog or moss land.
- *Mizzy*, SB. a soft, boggy place; allied to mist in mist-stall.
- *Out-rake* (N. Lanc.), SB. a common near enclosed land.
- *Parrock* (N. Lanc.), SB. an enclosure. A.S. *pearroc*.

- *Pingert, pingot,* SB. a small inclosure of land.
- *Pleck,* SB. a place.
- *Riggot,* SB. a narrow channel, a gutter.
- *Rindle,* SB. a small stream or brook. A.S. *rynel,* a stream or runnel.
- *Ryen,* SB. a narrow channel or footpath.
- *Sike,* SB. a drain, a gutter. Mid. E. *sike* (Stratmann); Icel. sík.
- *Skeer* (N. Lanc.), SB. a stone patch or bed on the sea-shore or on sand-banks.
- *Slack,* SB. a hollow place; a hollow between sand-hills on the coast. Also a depression between hills, corresponding with that which in Welsh is called a 'bwlch'. Icel. *slacki.*
- *Stanner* (Lytham), SB. a ridge of stones formed by the sea.
- *Swing,* ADJ. sloping. A swing-road has a ditch at one side only, and slopes uniformly towards the ditch, so that the top side is dry for foot passengers.
- *Syke,* SB. a ditch, a hollow place. Icel. *sík,* a gutter. In Yorkshire it is also a channel for water; also the current of water along a channel, which sometimes runs with great impetuosity down the side of a moor.
- *Trod,* SB. road, highway. Mid. E. *trod.*
- *Water-gait,* SB. a gully or reft in the rock, which in summer is the bed of a streamlet, but in winter is filled by a torrent.
- *Yearth,* SB. pron. of earth. The use of *y* before the vowel, as in this word, is very common in Lancashire. It also frequently takes the place of *h,* as in head, pronounced *yed.*
- *Yirth-bobs, yeth-bobs,* SB. pl. tufts of heath.
- *Yort,* SB. a yard, a fold.

- *Birk* (N. Lancs.), SB. a birch tree. A.S. *birce*; Icel. *björk*.
- *Blackbern*, SB. the blackberry.
- *Boof*, SB. the bough of a tree; also, the shaft of a cart.
- *Boortree* (S. Lanc.), *Bortree* (N. Lanc.), SB. the elder tree.
- *Bread-and-cheese*, SB. the leaves of the hawthorn. Also, in N. Lanc. the leaves and flowers of the *Oxalis acetosella*. A phrase used by children.
- *Brere*, SB. a briar. A.S. *brér*; Mid. E. *brere*. Names of places in Lancashire, Brerecliffe, Brerecroft.
- *Brog* (N. Lanc.), SB. a branch, a bough, a broken branch. Cf. W. *brigyn*, a top branch, a twig; *brigau*, the tops of trees.
- *Bulloe*, SB. the sloe or wild plum. W. *bwlas*, winter sloes.
- *Caff* (N. Lanc.), SB. chaff, refuse. A.S. *ceaf*; Du. *kaf*.
- *Chats*, SB. the catkins of the maple and other trees. Cf. *þe chattes of hasele. Voiage of Maundevile*, ed. Halliwell, p. 168. F. *chat*, a cat. *Catkin* is the dimin. of *cat*.
- *Chig* (Fylde), V. to remove the stalks from gooseberries.
- *Choup* (N. Lanc.), SB. the bright red fruit of the dog-rose (*Rosa canina*).
- *Churn* (N. Lanc.), SB. the daffodil.
- *Cloudberry*, SB. *Rubus chamæmorus*, which grows on Pendle – a semi-arctic plant, which Prof. Forbes considered to belong to the glacial era.
- *Cod*, SB. a husk, a pod of peas or beans. A.S. *codd*, a scrip, small bag; Sw. *kudde*, a sack, bag, pod; Icel. *koddi*, a pillow; W. *côd*, *cwd*, a bag or pouch.
- *Coke* (N. and E. Lanc.), SB. the pith of anything; the core of a fruit. Du. *kolk*, a pit, hollow, whirlpool; cf. Gael. *coach*, empty, hollow.
- *Cuckoo-meat*, SB. a large clover.
- *Cuckoo-spit*, SB. the froth found on grass or plants, enclosing an insect (*Cicada spumaria*).

- *Daffy-down-dilly*, SB. the daffodil.
- *Dead-tongue* (Furness), SB. the water hemlock.
- *Draff*, SB. malt grains after brewing. Icel. *draf*, husks, dregs; A.S. and Du. *drabbe*, dregs, lees.
- *Eggs-an'-collops*, SB. toad-flax (*Linaria vulgaris*).
- *Eisch-keys* (N. and Mid. Lanc.), SB. the pods containing the seed of the ash. A.S. *æsc*, ash-tree; whether the ending is really A.S. *cæg*, a key, is not proven.
- *Eshle-tree* (N. and E. Lanc.), SB. axle-tree. A.S. *eax*, an axle-tree, with the dimin. suffix el.
- *Fash*, SB. the leaves of a turnip or carrot. (Bamford's Glossary.)
- *Fayberry*, SB. Fairy's berry; a gooseberry.
- *Fellon-wood* (N. Lanc.), SB. the plant Bitter-sweet (*Solanum dulcamara*).
- *Fir-bob*, SB. a fir-cone.
- *Gale* (N. Lanc.), SB. the wild myrtle or bog-myrtle (*Myrica gale*).
- *Gaurdin* (Cartmel), SB. wood for hedging.
- *Gerse*, SB. grass.
- *Gilliver*, SB. the gilly-flower.
- *Gollin*, SB. the marsh marigold (*Caltha palustris*).
- *Goode* (N. Lanc.), SB. the ox-eye daisy (*Chrysanthemum leucanthemum*).
- *Goosegob*, SB. a gooseberry.
- *Gorrish, gorry*, ADJ. thick and luxuriant, sometimes coarse and luxuriant, applied to grass.
- *Green-sauce*, SB. a kind of sorrel with an acid flavour (*Rumex acetosa*).
- *Hagberry* (N. Lanc.), SB. the bird-cherry (*Prumus padus*).
- *Hague, haig*, SB. the hawthorn, but especially the hawthorn berry. Fruit of *Cratægus oxyacantha*. A.S. *haga*, a hedge, also *haw* or *hedge thorn*; *hagan, haws, fruit of the haw*, *hedge*, or

white thorn.

- *Hard-yeds*, SB. scabious; also called devil's-bit (*Scabiosa succisa*).
- *Hatch-horn*, SB. an acorn. Icel. *akarn*; A.S. *æcorn*.
- *Hattock*, SB. a corn sheaf.
- *Hollin*, SB. the holly. A.S. *holen*, *holegn*. The spellings *holin*, *holie* both occur in the *Ancren Riwle*, p. 418.
- *Horse-nop* (N. Lanc.), SB. the knap weed (*Centaurea nigra*).
- *Hull*, SB. a husk; used especially for the husk of a pea, which is called a pea-hull.
- *Ivin*, SB. ivy.
- *Jinny-green-teeth*, SB. literally the green scum on ponds, but supposed to imply the presence of a water-sprite or 'boggart'; a terror to children as they pass the pond on which the appearance is seen.
- *Kecks*, *Kex*, SB. pl. the hollow stems of the common hemlock; used by lads to shoot peas with, also for making a rude flageolet.
- *Keddle-dock*, SB. common ragwort (*Senecio jacobæa*).
- *Keish* (N. Lanc.), SB. the hollow stem of the hemlock.
- *Krindle*, SB. kernel.
- *Ladsavvur*, *lads-love*, SB. southernwood (*Artemisia abrotanum*).
- *Lady-smock*, SB. the plant cuckoo-flower (*Cardamine pratensis*). Most commonly known in Lancashire as the 'May-flower'.
- *Leem* (N. Lanc.), V. to free nuts from their husks.
- *Leemers* (N. Lanc.), SB. ripe hazel nuts.
- *May-flower*, SB. the lady-smock (*Cardamine pratensis*).
- *Moss-crop*, SB. cotton-grass (*Eriophorum*).
- *Nap-at-noon* (N. Lanc.), SB. the purple goat's-beard (*Trapogon porrifolius*, Linnæus), which opens its flowers only

in the forenoon, after which they close.

- *Owler*, SB. the alder; alder timber.
- *Paddock-stool*, SB. a fungus, a toad-stool.
- *Payshun-dock*, SB. patience-dock or passion-dock; called also poor-man's cabbage.
- *Pea-swad*, SB. the hull or husk of a pea.
- *Pignut*, SB. the earth-nut (*Bunium flexiosum*).
- *Pissabed*, SB. the dandelion flower.
- *Posset*, SB. the flower of the meadow-sweet.
- *Ragged-robin*, SB. the meadow-lychnis (*Lychnis flos-cuculi*).
- *Ramps* (N. Lanc.), SB. wild onions (*Allium ursinum*). Short for *ramsons*.
- *Robin-run-i'-th-hedge*, SB. the plant bedstraw (*Gallium*).
- *Sawgh*, SB. a willow. A.S. *sealh*, cognate with (not derived from) Lat. *salix*.
- *Scrunt*, SB. brushwood, stunted undergrowth.
- *Shude*, SB. the husk of grain, chaff.
- *Shull*, SB. the husk or integument.
- *Skedlock*, SB. charlock, a weed which grows among corn and in waste places (*Sinapis arvensis*).
- *Sour-dock*, SB. meadow sorrel (*Rumex acetosa*).
- *Swad*, SB. a husk or shell. Cf. E. *swathe*.
- *Tang* (Lytham), SB. a long tongue-like seaweed. Danish *tang*; Icel. *þang*.
- *Tangle*, SB. seaweed. Icel. *þöngull*.
- *Whicks*, SB. pl. quicks, thorns.
- *Wicken*, SB. the mountain ash, the rowan tree of Scotland. At Seal-Bank, near Greenfield, Saddleworth, there is a place called the Wicken-hole, from the abundance of trees of this kind growing there.
- *Winberry, wimberry*, SB. the whortleberry (*Vaccinium myrtillus*). A.S. *win-berige*; lit. wine-berry, from the

resemblance to a diminutive grape.

- *Windles*, SB. pl. blades of grass, or corn, or anything blown astray by the wind.
- *Windlestraw*, SB. coarse, wiry grass.
- *Winrow*, SB. a row of hay in the meadow: wind-row.
- *Wythins* (*y* long), SB. pl. osiers, withies.
- *Wyzel* (*y* long), SB. the haulm or stalk of the potato.
- *Yarb*, SB. herb; also occasionally used for hay-grass.

- *Beck-bibby* (Furness), SB. the water-ousel. For *bibby* cf. Lat. *bibo*, to drink, and Mid. E. *bibble*, to sip, to tipple.
- *Bitter-bump*, SB. the bittern (*Botaurus stellaris*). The syllable bump refers to the booming sound made by it. The Welsh name is *aderyn y bwmp*, the booming bird. 'The bittern is now rare in Britain, owing to drainage. It has a peculiar bellowing cry, which has obtained for it such English provincial names as Mire-drum, Bull-of-the-Bog, etc., and many of its appellations in other languages, as Bitour, Botur, Botaurus.' (Chambers's Encyclopaedia, vol. II.)
- *Black-clock*, SB. the cockroach or black-beetle; more commonly called *twitch-clock*.
- *Black-ousel*, SB. the blackbird (*Turdus merula*).
- *Bracken-clock* (Furness), SB. a small beetle.
- *Brid*, SB. a bird. A.S. *brid*.
- *Brock*, SB. a badger, from the white-streaked face of the animal. Names of places in Lancashire, Brockholes, Brocksbottom. Gael. *broice*, a mole, a freckle; *brucach*, spotted; *breac*, speckled; W. *brech*, *brych*, brindled, freckled; Icel. *brokkr*, a badger; Dan. *brok*, a badger; A.S. *broc*.
- *Brog*, *broggle*, V. to fish for eels by making the water muddy.
- *Bull-heads*, *bull-jones*, SB. tadpoles.
- *Bummel-bee*, SB. the humble-bee. W. *bwmp*, a hollow sound.
- *Buzzert*, SB. a moth or butterfly, the cockchafer. Mr. Wedgwood says: 'The name buzzard is given to a beetle from the buzzing sound of its flight, and it is to be thus understood in the expression blind buzzard. We also say, as blind as a beetle, as heedless as a cockchafer, from the blind way in which they fly against one.' On the other hand, it is certain that bosarde in the *Rom. of Rose*, 4033, meant a hawk; O. Fr. *busard*. Mr. Wedgwood's suggestion lacks proof.
- *Chitty* (E. and N. Lanc.), SB. a cat; also, the wren, commonly

called *chitty-wer-wren*.

- *Chitty* (S. Lanc.), SB. the lesser red-poll linnet. In Manchester and the suburbs it is also called the *greybob*.
- *Cleg*, SB. the gadfly. Icel. *kleggi*, the horse-fly.
- *Clock*, SB. a beetle: generally used with a descriptive prefix, as *bracken-clock*, *black-clock*, *twitch-clock*, and so forth. The entry 'chuleich, scarabæus' occurs in an O.H. German gloss. See Garnett's Essays, p. 68. No such word as clock is to be found in A.S. dictionaries.
- *Con* (N. Lanc.), SB. a squirrel. Cf. E. *coney*, a rabbit.
- *Corby*, SB. a carrion crow; the raven. Mid. E. *corbyal*; Lat. *corvus*; Icel. *korpr*; Sw. *korp*; O. Fr. *corbel*.
- *Craa* (N. Lanc.), SB. crow.
- *Cronk*, SB. the note of a raven. Also, croaking, prating. Icel. *krúnk*, the raven's cry, *krúnka*, to croak.
- *Culver*, SB. the dove or pigeon. A.S. *culfre*.
- *Cushy-cow-lady*, SB. the lady-bird or lady-fly; *coccinella*.
- *Easin-sparrow*, SB. the common house-sparrow.
- *Edder* (S. Lanc.), *Edther* (N. Lanc), *Etherd* (E. Lanc.), SB. an adder. Mid. O.E. *addre*, *eddre* probably: *naddre*, *neddre*. A.S. *næddre*, *nædre*; etym. disputed.
- *Edderbowt*, *edtherbowt*, SB. the dragon-fly. See *Edder*, *Edther* + *bolt*.
- *Eddercrop*, *Edthercrop*, SB. a spider. Formed like A.S. *átter-coppa*, a spider, with a variation in the second part. It is therefore from A.S. *átter*, poison, and *crop*, a top, or bunch, alluding to the supposed poison bag.
- *Egg-clock*, SB. a cockchafer.
- *Eslins* (N. and E. Lanc.), SB. a salmon-fly.
- *Fleck*, SB. a flea.
- *Foomert, foomart*, SB. a martin, polecat, or fitchew. Mid. E. *folmart*. Prof Skeat (Etym. Dictionary) says 'A hybrid

compound; Mid. E. *ful* = A.S. *fúl*, foul, ſtinking; and old French *marte*, *martre*, a marten. Thus it means "foul marten."'

- *Frog-rud*, SB. the ſpawn of the frog, which may often be seen floating on ſtagnant pools or ditches.
- *Frosk* (N. Lanc.), SB. a frog. A.S. *forx*; Icel. *froskr*.
- *Fud* (N. Lanc.), SB. the hair of a hare or rabbit.
- *Garden-twod*, SB. a large toad.
- *Gillhooter*, SB. an owl.
- *Glead*, SB. a hawk.
- *Goldſpink*, *gowdſpink*, (Mid. and W. Lanc.), SB. a goldfinch.
- *Goor* (W. Lanc.), SB. a seagull.
- *Gowk* (W. Lanc.), SB. the cuckoo.
- *Greeney* (N. Lanc.), SB. the green grosbeak, or green linnet.
- *Hagworm* (N. Lanc.), SB. the common snake; lit. *hedgeworm*.
- *Horse-ſtang* (N. Lanc.), SB. the gad-fly.
- *Hullet*, SB. an owl.
- *Hully-butterflee* (N. Lanc.), SB. any heavy-bodied night-flying moth.
- *Hummabee*, SB. the common field bee; a hummer-bee.
- *Jammy-crane* (N. Lanc.), SB. the heron.
- *Jinny-ſpinner* (N. Lanc.), SB. an inſect (Tipula).
- *Ket-crow* (Fylde and Lonsdale), SB. the carrion crow.
- *Layrock*, *learock*, SB. the lark. Icel. *lævirki*. Chaucer in *Cant. Tales* has *laverock*; *Romaunt of Rose*, 1. 662, *laverokkes*; Burns, *Holy Fair*, ſt. 1.
- *Mack* (N. Lanc.), SB. a maggot. Mid. E. *mawk*.
- *Moth-ullet* (Lytham), SB. a small butterfly: moth-owlet.
- *Mowdywarp*, SB. the mole. Icel. *moldvarpa*.
- *Neet-haak* (N. Lanc.), SB. the night-jar (*Caprimulgus europæus*).
- *Ouzel*, SB. the blackbird.
- *Paddock*, SB. the toad or frog. Icel. *padda*.

- *Peet-lark*, the meadow-pipit or titlark (*Anthus pratensis*).
- *Pismote*, sb. an ant. Cf. A.S. *maða*, a maggot, a bug.
- *Pyanet* (N. Lanc.), *Pynart* (S. Lanc.), *Pynot* (general), *Pyot* (Cartmel), sb. a magpie.
- *Sea-nee*, sb. a small fresh-water eel.
- *Shepster*, sb. the starling. So named from settling on sheep's backs.
- *Tewit*, sb. the lapwing or green plover (*Vanellus cristatus*).
- *Tinge*, sb. a small red bug.
- *Tullet* (Fylde), sb. a small gull.
- *Twitch-clock*, sb. the common black beetle.
- *Ullert, ullet*, sb. a young owl, owlet. A.S. *úle*, an owl.
- *Urchin*, sb. a hedgehog.
- *Yad, Yaud*, (N. Lanc.), sb. a horse. Cf. E. *jade*.
- *Yallow-yorin'* (N. Lanc.), sb. the Yellow-Bunting or Yellow-Hammer (*Emberiza citrinella*).

- *Battin*, SB. a bundle of ſtraw.
- *Bauks*, SB. pl. as SB. sing., a hayloft. For *balks*; from A.S. *balca*, a beam. The use of the plural is easily explained; the loft would be between the balks or rafters.
- *Beeas*, SB. beaſts, cattle. The plural of beaſt, formed by dropping the *t*, the plural *s* not having been suffixed.
- *Beeſt, Beeſtins, Beeas-milk* (N. Lanc.), SB. the firſt milk after calving. A.S. *byſting*, the same; from A.S. *beoſt*, the same. Cf. Ger. *bieſt-milch*.
- *Bigg* (Furness), SB. barley. Icel. *bygg*, barley.
- *Billet*, SB. a piece of wood pointed at each end, used in farming. Fr. *billot*, a block; dim. of *bille*, a log, of Celtic origin. Cf, Irish *bille*, a tree-trunk (Brachet).
- *Boon-ploo* (N. Lanc.) SB. a day's ploughing given to each other by neighbouring farmers, or to the lord of the manor, or by a sub-tenant to the holder of the land. From *boon* and *plough*.
- *Boon-shearin'* (N. Lanc.), SB. a quantity of shearing given as in the case of a *boon-ploo*.
- *Boose, booſt*, SB. a cattle-ſtall. Often used for the upper part of the ſtall where the fodder is placed: as 'Yo'll find it in th' cow's boose.' Figuratively, a seat. A.S. *bós, bósig*, a ſtall, manger, crib.
- *Boskin*, SB. a cattle-ſtall. From *boose*, with the suffix *kin*.
- *Boſtin'* (mid. Lanc.), SB. the rack or trough in a ſtable, in which the fodder is placed.
- *Bullart*, SB. the warden of a bull; lit. a bull-ward.
- *Byre*, SB. a cowhouse. A.S. *búr*; Icel. *búr*.
- *Camril, Cammerel* (Fylde), SB. the lower part of a horse's leg. Cf. W. *cambren*, a crooked ſtick. Mid. E. *gambrel*, a bent ſtick; from *cam*, crooked.
- *Churn-gettin'* (S. Lanc.), SB. a night feaſt after harveſt.

- *Clam-rattan* (N. Lanc.), ADJ. app. to a farm where the soil is poor or unproductive. See *Clem*.
- *Clam-stave-an'-daub*, SB. a combination of clay or mud and sticks, used in the making of walls. A.S. *clam*, clay, and *stæf*, a staff or stick.
- *Cleavin'* (Cartmel), SB. the last furrow in ploughing.
- *Clem* (S. Lanc), *Clam* (E. Mid. and N. Lanc.), V. to starve from want of food. Du. *klemmen*, to pinch; O.L. German *(bi-)klemman*; O.H. German *(bi-)chlemmen*, to clam; Du. *kleumen*, to be benumbed with cold.
- *Clewkin'-grin*, SB. a game-snare, made of twine. *Clewkin* (which see), and A.S. *grin*, a snare. A grin is the true Mid.E. form; corrupted to *gin*, from confusion with engine.
- *Cloak'n* (S. Lanc.), *Coakin* (E. Lanc.), SB. the sharp part or cramp of a horse-shoe. E. *calkin*.
- *Cooter*, SB. pron. of *coulter*, a ploughshare.
- *Corn-boggart*, SB. a scare-crow, set up to frighten birds from the wheat.
- *Cow-grip*, SB. a trench in a shippon, to carry off the water.
- *Cree*, V. to soften wheat, barley or rice by simmering.
- *Crow-boggart*, SB. a scare-crow.
- *Cush, Cushy*, SB. a child's name for a cow. Icel. *kussa*, a cow; *kus*, a word used to call cows.
- *Dag*, V. to shear sheep. Mid. E. *daggen*, to cut into jagged edges. The expression 'leet dagge his clothes' in *Piers the Plowman*, B. XX. 142, means 'he caused his clothes to be curiously cut' in allusion to the fashion of the period.
- *Daglocks*, SB. pl. the wool cut off a sheep.
- *Daub, Dobe*, SB. clay or marl; also, the clay mixed with chopped straw, formerly used for filling in between the timbers of wooden-framed houses, sometimes called 'wattle and daub'.

- *Daub-hoil*, SB. i.e. daub-hole; a clay or marl pit.
- *Dess* (Fylde), SB. a pile, appl. to straw. Icel. *des*, a rick, whence *hey-des*, a hay-rick. It exists in local names, as *Desjur-myri* in the east, *Des-ey* in the west of Iceland.
- *Doytch-back*, SB. (i.e. ditch back), a fence, a rampart above a ditch.
- *Ealin'*, SB. a shed set against another building; a lean-to. Lit. a heeling, from the verb to heel or lean over. *Heel* is a corruption from Mid. E. *helden*, A.S. *hyldan*, to incline. See *Helden* in Stratmann, and *Heel* in Wedgwood.
- *Easins*, SB. the eaves of a house; also applied to sloping land. Thus Habergham-Eaves: Habergham slopes (properly slope, as eaves is singular). For *evesings*, from A.S. *efesung*, a shearing round from the verb *efesian*, to shave round; which from A.S. *efese*, a brim, edge, margin. Mid. E. *evesunge*, *evesinge*.
- *Eddish* or *Edditch*, SB. the first grass after mowing. A.S. *edisc*, aftermath, where prefix *ed* = again. Mid. E. *edisch*.
- *Elder*, SB. the cow's udder.
- *Enty* (N. Lanc.), SB. the last furrow in a rigg. A.S. *ende*; Icel. *endi*, the end, conclusion.
- *Fadge*, SB. a burden, part of a horse's load. (Bamford's Glossary.)
- *Fellon* (N. Lanc.), SB. a sore, a disease in cows.
- *Fey*, V. to remove the earth over stone or slate.
- *Flaight*, SB. a light turf.
- *Flay-crow* (N. Lanc.), SB. a scarecrow, a ridiculous object. Pronounced: *Flay-craa*.
- *Fog*, SB. the later growth of grass; the aftermath.
- *Fold, fowd, fowt*, SB. a cluster of houses.
- *Foor* (N. Lanc.), SB. a furrow.
- *Frampit* (Ormskirk), *Famput* (S.E. Lanc.), SB. an iron which slides on the boose-stake to fasten cows in their stall.

- *Gait* (N. Lanc.), SB. pasturage for cattle during summer in a common field.
- *Gaitins* (N. Lanc.), SB. pl. single sheaves of corn set up on end to dry.
- *Gang* (Cartmel), SB. a lobby in a farm-house.
- *Gang-boose*, SB. a narrow passage from the cow-house to the barn. See *Boose*. A.S. *gang*, a way, path, passage.
- *Garth* (N. Lanc.), SB. a small field or enclosure adjoining a house, church, or other building; usually an affix, as *school-garth*, *church-garth*, *chapel-garth*. W. *gardd*, an enclosure.
- *Gersins*, SB. moorland pastures.
- *Gildert* (N. Lanc.), SB. a snare of horse-hair.
- *Gimmer* (N. Lanc.), SB. a two-year old sheep.
- *Gise* (*g* soft; N. Lanc.), V. to put cattle out to grass at a sum agreed upon per head.
- *Gist* (*g* soft; N. Lanc.), V. to pasture out cattle upon hire.
- *Gistin'* (N. Lanc.), SB. the pasturage of cattle at a price.
- *Grip-yard*, *grip-yort*, SB. a platting of stakes and twisted boughs filled up with earth; generally made to confine a water-course, and occasionally to form artificial banks and seats in pleasure gardens.
- *Groop*, SB. a channel in a shippon behind the cows.
- *Gyrr*, V. to purge. A *gyrrd cauve* is a calf purged by having had too rich milk.
- *Hadloont* (E. Lanc.), SB. pronunciation of *Adlant*; the headland of a ploughed field.
- *Hadloont-reean*, SB. the gutter, ditch, or space between the head lands and others.
- *Hamshackle*, V. to fasten the head of a vicious animal to one of its forelegs.
- *Hawmbark*, SB. a horse-collar.
- *Hawms* (Ormskirk), SB. pl. the hames, the part of the collar

by which horses draw. Pronun. of 'hame'. 'Hame and chain maker' common in Manchester.

- *Hay*, V. to lay bare; to remove the top earth off gravel.
- *Haybant*, SB. a twisted band of hay.
- *Hay-moo*, SB. a stack of hay. *Moo* is the pronunciation of *mow*, which means the pile or stack of hay which had been mowed. A *mow* is also the loft or chamber in which hay or corn is laid up. The 'Barley Mow' is an alehouse sign in Manchester.
- *Hempland* (N. Lanc.), SB. a small piece of land set apart for growing flax for family use. Mr. J. P. Morris says the practice has fallen into disuse, but the patches of land still retain the name.
- *Henridge, hainridge, haining-ground*, (Ormskirk), SB. an outlet for cattle.
- *Hog*, V. to cover a heap with earth or straw.
- *Hog-mutton*, SB. a year-old sheep.
- *Jambles*, SB. the *hames*; the part of the collar by which horses draw.
- *Joyst*, SB. pasturage for cattle let out to farmers or others for a consideration. A corruption of *agist*.
- *Kestlin*, SB. a calf dropped before its time.
- *Kye*, SB. pl. cows, kine. A.S. *cú*, a cow; *cy*, cows.
- *Laith, leath*, SB. a barn or storehouse. Icel. *hlaða*, a barn, a storehouse.
- *Langel* (N. Lanc.), SB. to tie the forelegs of cattle to prevent them from straying.
- *Lea* (N. Lanc.), SB. a scythe. Icel. *lé, ljár*.
- *Leaf*, SB. the inner fat of the pig, which, when melted, is called lard.
- *Lickin'*, SB. provender for cattle.
- *Lonk*, SB. a Lancashire-bred sheep.

- *Lowk* (Fylde and N. Lanc.), v. to weed. Icel. *lok*, a weed; A.S. *lyccan*, to pull, weed.
- *Mawkin*, sb. a scarecrow. *Rob-mawkin* is a poor fellow who exchanges his hat or coat for that which has been used for a scarecrow.
- *Midden*, sb. a heap of dung or refuse; the ash pit at one time commonly attached to most houses in Lancashire. Dan. *mödding*, a dunghill.
- *Mistal*, sb. a cowhouse: mist-stall; mist = dung.
- *Mow*, v. to cover up, to heap together.
- *Mull*, *mullocks*, (Fylde), sb. broken turf.
- *Muse*, sb. a gap for game; a run in a hedge for rabbits or other game. O. Fr. *mussette*.
- *Pant* (Cartmel), sb. mud.
- *Pantle* (Fylde), sb. a bird-snare made of hair. O.Fr. *pantiere*, a kind of snare for birds.
- *Pantle* (Ormskirk), v. to snare for snipes.
- *Pluck*, sb. the lungs of a sheep, cow, or other animal.
- *Pytch*, sb. a hive for bees. Probably cognate with 'pitch' of a roof, or 'pitch' a covering of anything as a defence against weather. A breakwater is said to be 'pitched' with stones on the surface.
- *Rook*, *ruck*, sb. a heap, a number together, a lot.
- *Shippon*, sb. a place for housing cattle. A.S. *scypen*, the same.
- *Skarn*, sb. dung. Icel. *skarn*.
- *Skelboose*, sb. a passage by the side of a cattle stall, made so that a man can get to the fodder-rack in front of the cattle.
- *Stoop*, sb. a stump.
- *Sweelin'*, v. firing the heather on the moors in winter.
- *Thick-neck* (Heysham), sb. a false growth in corn; the growing of several stalks together.
- *Thrinter*, sb. a three-year-old sheep.

- *Thwite*, *thwittle*, v. to cut. A.S. *thwítan*, to cut.
- *Thwittle*, SB. a knife. Cf. Icel. *þveita*, *þvita*, a kind of axe or chopper.
- *Twinter*, SB. a two-year-old sheep. Lit. two-winter.
- *Wye-cauve*, SB. a she-calf.
- *Yedders* (N. Lanc.), SB. pl. wattling bands for hedges.
- *Yower* (N. Lanc.), SB. the udder of a cow. Icel. *júgr*.

- *Bass*, SB. iron pyrites or shale, found in coal; coal which will not burn.
- *Beet*, V. to kindle or amend a fire. A.S. *bétan*, to amend, to better; also to kindle a fire. Cf. Sc. *beet*, to kindle. From the root of better.
- *Blash*, SB. a sudden flame. A variation of blaze; A.S. *blo'ese*.
- *Blash-boggart*, SB. a fire-goblin, or flash-goblin; that is, a goblin that flashes and disappears. It is more commonly used figuratively, and is applied to persons who are fiery, wild, or strange in appearance, either in dress or person.
- *Chats*, *Chatwood*, SB. small twigs for lighting fires.
- *Eldin'* (N. Lanc.), *Eildin'* (N., Mid. and S. Lanc.), SB. fuel or fire. The word is appl. to any kind of fuel, and to the brushwood of which fences are made. Icel. *elding*, firing, fuel; Scot. *eilding*, from Icel. *eldr*, fire; A.S. *æled*, fire; A.S. *ælan*, to kindle.
- *Ess* (S. and S.E. Lanc. and Goosnargh dist.), SB. ashes. A.S. *asce*, *ásce*; Icel. *aska*; Mid. E. *asche*, *esche*, *esse*.
- *Ess-hole* (S. and S.E. Lanc.), SB. a hole under the fire which receives the ashes.
- *Grummel*, SB. pl. small coal, riddlings.
- *Ingle-nook*, SB. the corner of a fire-place.
- *Keen*, V. to kindle.
- *Naplins*, SB. pl. small round coal, as distinguished from the cob and slack or dust. Also, 'nibblins'.
- *Rake*, V. to cover or heap up a fire with coals or cinders in order to keep it alive.
- *Slack*, SB. small coals.
- *Slack*, V. to cover the fire with small coals so as to make consumption slow.
- *Sleck*, SB. small fine coal.
- *Teend*, V. to light, to kindle. A.S. *tendan*, *tyndan*, to set fire to. Icel. *tendra*, to make a fire, to light.

- *Ark*, SB. a press to keep clothes in; a large chest for holding meal or flour. About Oldham and Hollinwood *ark* is a repository. The country 'badger' (q.v.) or provision-dealer will say *malt-ark, flour-ark, meal-ark*, and so on. A.S. *arc, earc*, a coffer, chest, vessel.
- *Bearin'*, SB. a weaver's burden, usually applied to the week's work when taken back to the employer.
- *Beetins*, SB. pl. short lengths of yarn, used by weavers to piece up broken ends in a warp. Possibly for *beetings*, i.e. mendings; from Mid. E. *bete*, to mend.
- *Beetlin'-steän* (Furness), SB. Pron. of beetling-stone; a stone upon which clothes are *beetled* or beaten.
- *Beggar-inkle*, SB. a coarse, narrow tape, hawked by beggars. Of *inkle*, Wedgwood says: Fr. *ligneul, lignol*, strong threads; O.E. *liniolf. Lynyolf* or *inniolf*, threde to sow with schone or botys; indula, licinium (Prompt. Parv.). The loss of the inital *l*, of which we have here an example, would convert *lingle* into *ingle* or *inkle*.
- *Bunhorns*, SB. pl. briars to wind yarn on.
- *Chean* (S. Lanc.), SB. a woollen warp.
- *Clewkin*, SB. twine, string. A.S. *cliwe*, a clew, hank; Mid. E. *cleowe*.
- *Clout*, SB. a piece of cloth used for domestic purposes, as dish-clout; a patch of leather or iron. A.S. *clút*, a little cloth; Mid. E. *clout, clutian, clutien*, to patch. Icel. *klutr*, a kerchief. Dan. *klud*, W. *clwt*.
- *Cockers*, SB. pl. stockings; hose without feet. A.S. *cocer*, a sheath; Du. *koker*, a sheath, case, quiver.
- *Cop*, SB. a small oval-shaped bundle of spun cotton thread, prepared in that form for the manufacturer of cloth. W. *cob*, a tuft.
- *Copster*, SB. a spinner. See *Cop*. Cf. W. *cob*, a tuft; also, a spider.

- *Creel*, SB. a frame to wind yarn upon.
- *Cut*, SB. a weaver's term for a piece of calico when taken from the loom.
- *Deawnt*, V. finished; taken off or taken down. *Deawin'*, finishing, PT. Lancashire weavers call the web, or piece of cloth they are working upon, whether woollen or cotton, a 'cut'; and when the entire piece of web is woven, and taken off the loom, the weaver says he has 'deawnt his cut'; that is, he has taken his finished web down from the loom. So, figuratively, a man who dies has finished the web of his life.
- *Deet* (S. Lanc.), V. to dress with size or paste; a term used by weavers.
- *Gate*, V. to begin; to put a loom in order for working.
- *Gooer, Gore*, SB. a triangular piece of cloth stitched into a shirt or other garment when greater width is required at one end than at the other.
- *Lease, leece*, SB. the dividing of the thread in a warp.
- *Leece-rod*, SB. a rod to divide the threads of a warp.
- *Lindrins*, SB. pl. ropes put round a weaver's beam when the woof is nearly finished.
- *Linther*, V. to make fast the end of a warp so that it can be woven close and finished.
- *Pickin'-peg, pickin'-rod, pickin'-stick*, SB. a wooden rod or handle by which the shuttle is thrown in weaving.
- *Slay*, SB. the hand-board of a loom.
- *Slivvin*, SB. a number of hanks of yarn put together.
- *Swingin'-stick*, SB. a hazel stick for beating wool. In the cotton manufacture the same thing was called a *battin'-stick*.
- *Thrums*, SB. pl. the ends of a warp. Icel. *þrömr*, an edge.
- *Webster*, SB. a weaver. Mid. E. *webstere*.

- *Bain* (N. Lanc.), ADV. near, adjacent, convenient. Icel. *beinn*, direct; *beint*, straight.
- *Burly-man*, SB. an officer appointed at court leet to examine and determine respecting disputed fences.
- *Byng*, V. to bewitch.
- *Cammed* (S. Lanc.), *Caimt* (N. and E. Lanc.), ADJ. and ADV. crooked; also, bad-tempered, ill-natured. W. *cam*, crooked; *camu*, to bend.
- *Cank*, V. to talk, to chatter. Cf. Icel. *kank*, gibes; *kankast*, V. to jeer, gibe.
- *Cart-swoe* (Fylde), SB. the rut made by a cartwheel. Cf. A.S. *swæth*, a track.
- *Catter*, V. to lay up money, to thrive. Cf. Sc. *cater*, money; Eng. *cater*, to provide; O. Fr. *acater*; Fr. *acheter*.
- *Chunner*, V. to grumble in a low tone, to murmur.
- *Clack*, V. to chatter. Icel. *klaka*, to twitter, to chatter.
- *Clam* (N. Lanc.), V. to dry up, to clog up. A.S. *clám*, a bandage; also clay.
- *Clashy* (N. Lanc.), ADJ. wet and uncomfortable, as applied to weather.
- *Clom, Clomb, Clōme, Clum*, V. climbed.
- *Cockle*, V. to wrinkle. Properly, like *coggle, joggle*, to shake or jerk up and down, then applied to a surface thrown into hollows and projections by partial shaking, by unequal contraction. A cockling sea is one jerked up into short waves by contrary currents (Wedgwood).
- *Cop*, SB. the top or head of anything. A.S. *copp*, W. *cop*, the head, top, apex. O. Fris. *kop*, the head.
- *Cow-quakes* (Fylde), SB. pl. cold winds in May.
- *Cronky*, ADJ. rough, uneven.
- *Crookelt, Croot*, ADJ. Du. *kreukelen*, to crumple; Platt Deutsch *krukeln*.

- *Crovukt* (N. Lanc.), ADJ. crushed up, crowded. W. *crybwch*, shrunk.
- *Crowd*, SB. a fiddle. W. *crwth*, a fiddle.
- *Dacker*, ADJ. unsettled; generally applied to the weather.
- *Dark*, ADJ. blind.
- *Darkenin'*, SB. twilight. A.S. *dearcung*, twilight.
- *Dawk* (Fylde), *Deawk* (S. and E. Lancs.), V. to stoop, to plunge. Lit. to duck. Cf. Du. *duiken*, to stoop, dive, plunge.
- *Deave*, V. to deafen; to stupefy with noise. ADJ. *Deavin*, deafening. Icel. *deyfa*, to stupefy; O. Sw. *dofwa*, to deafen, dull, assuage, stupefy; Dan. *döve*, to deafen, deaden, blunt.
- *Deawn-broo*, ADV. down hill, metaph. for falling or declining.
- *Deg*, V. to sprinkle water upon anything. Icel. *döggva*, to bedew; cf. Icel. *deigja*, wetness, damp; Sw. *dagg*, dew.
- *Doage*, *Doych* (E. Lanc.), ADJ. damp. A.S. *deawig*, dewy, wet.
- *Eaver* (sometimes *Ether*), SB. a quarter of the heavens, as 'the wind is in a rainy eaver'.
- *Eawl-leet* (pron. of *Owl-light*), SB. twilight.
- *Edge-o'-dark*, SB. twilight.
- *Ee-bree*, SB. the eyebrow. A.S. *eáge*, eye, and *bræw*, brow.
- *Ee*, SB. the eye; *Een*, pl. A.S. *eáge*, pl. *eágan*.
- *Fleet-time* (Ormskirk), SB. break of day, twilight.
- *Flinders*, SB. pl. small pieces, fragments.
- *Flusk*, SB. a whirring sound.
- *Fore-end*, SB. early spring; the beginning of a thing or time; used as the opposite of far-end.
- *Glent*, SB. a glance, a quick view.
- *Gliff* (N. Lanc.), SB. a glimpse, a transient sight.
- *Glime* (N. Lanc.), V. to glance aside, to look askance.
- *Glisk*, V. to glitter, shine, sparkle, glisten.
- *Glizzen*, V. to sparkle.
- *Glizzen*, SB. lightning.

- *GodŠtone*, SB. a small, round, white Štone found by children and kept in the pocket as something valuable.
- *Greese*, SB. Štairs, Šteps; also a little brow, an ascent. Latimer has 'greesings', meaning Šteps.
- *Grun-gron*, ADJ. grown on the ground; a native of a given locality; homeŠþun.
- *Halliblash*, SB. a great blaze; something which dazzles.
- *Hammil*, SB. a hamlet. A.S. *ham*, a home, dwelling, village.
- *Hammil-scoance*, SB. the lantern or light of the village; the village of Solomon.
- *Heck* (N. Lanc.), SB. a half-door or hatch; a gate.
- *Kizen't* (N. Lanc.), ADJ. parched, dried up.
- *Lant*, SB. Štale urine. Generally Šþoke of as 'owd lant'. Formerly much used by Lancashire cottagers for scouring or cleaning blankets and other woollen cloths; also for sundry medicinal purposes. In every yard or garden would have been found a receptacle for Štoring it. Icel. *hland*.
- *Low*, SB. a flame. Icel. *log*, a flame.
- *Main-shore*, SB. the principal sewer in a Štreet.
- *Owl-leet*, SB. twilight.
- *Rag*, SB. hoar froŠt.
- *Rubbin'-Štone*, SB. a small Štone used for scouring and whitening the flagged floors of cottages.
- *Scorrick*, SB. a fragment, a crumb.
- *Screed*, SB. a shred, a fragment. A.S. *screáde*, a shred.
- *Skew* (Ormskirk), V. to fly sideways. A hawk skews about.
- *Underbree* (N. Lanc.), SB. a bright light appearing under clouds.
- *Wicken-whistle*, SB. a whiŠtle made out of a piece of the mountain-ash, the tender bark of which is easily manipulated.
- *Wrythen*, PT. ADJ. twiŠted, gnarled. A.S. *wriðen*, p.p. of the Štrong verb *wríðan*, to writhe.

ABBREVIATIONS

A.S.	Anglo-Saxon
Dan.	Danish
Du.	Dutch
E.	English dialect
Fr.	French
Gael.	Gaelic
Ger.	German
Icel.	Icelandic
Lat.	Latin
Mid. E.	Middle English
Mid. O.E.	Middle Old English
Mœs.-Goth.	Mœso-Gothic
O. Fr.	Old French
O. Fris	Old Frisian
O.H. German	Old High German
O.L. German	Old Low German
O. Sw.	Old Swedish
Sc.	Scottish
Suio-Goth.	Suio-Gothic
Sw.	Swedish
W.	Welsh

FARM NAMES

FROM CENSUS RECORDS

The census records provide a fascinating, if incomplete, picture of the old farms of Rivington and Anglezarke.

The information that follows has been sourced from various transcripts, rather than orginal documents, and therefore may be subject to error.

In collating these sources I have no doubt introduced further errors, although I have attempted at all times to preserve the spellings as I found them. Some show marked variations – for example, in 1841, Old Rachel's is listed as Old Rackets.

CENSUS STREET INDEX, ANGLEZARKE

(1841)	(1851)
....	....
Brooks	Brooks
Brock House	....
Coppice	....
Foggs	Foggs
Gurnest	....
High Bulloughs	High Bulloughs
....	....
....	....
Higher Henshaws	....
....	....
Jepsons	Jepsons
....	....
Lester Mill	....
Lees	Widow Lees
Lee House	....
....	Lower Andertons
....	....
....	....
....	....
Parsons Bulloughs	Parsons Bulloughts
Siddons Fold	....
....	....
....	....
Simms	Simms
Snapes	Snapes
Stones House	Stones House
....	....
White Coppice	White Coppice
....	....
....	....
Wilkinsons Bulloughs	Wilkinson Bulloughts

(1871)	(1891)
....	Albion Villa
....	....
Brook House	Brook House Farm
....	....
Foggs Farm	Foggs Farm
Gernest Farm	Garnesh
High Bullough Cottage	High Ballough
Bulloughs Farm	Ballough Farm
Bulloughs Cottage	....
....	....
Huts, The	....
Jepsons Farm	Jepsons Farm
Jepsons Cottage	....
....	....
....	....
Lea, The	Lee House
....	....
Lower Hempshaws Farm	....
Mines Cottage	....
....	Nightingales
....	....
Siddow Fold Farm	Siddow Fold
Siddow Fold Cottage	....
Siddow Fold House	....
Simms Farm	....
....	Snapes Farm
Stones House Cottage	Stones House
Waterworks Cottage	Water House
White Coppice House	White Coppice
White Coppice Farm	White Coppice Farm
White Coppice Cottage	....
Wilkinsons Bullough	....

CENSUS STREET INDEX, RIVINGTON

(1871)	(1891)
Acre, The	....
Ainsworths	Ainsworths
....	....
Alders, The	....
Andertons	Andertons
Beech House	Beech House
Beech Lodge	....
....	....
....	....
Public House	Public House
....	....
Bowmans	....
Bradleys	Bradleys
....	....
Brownhill	Brown Hill Farm
....	....
....	....
Castle	....
....	....
....	....
Coomp	....
Crambo	Crambo
Croft Gates	....
Crosses Cottage	....
Crosses	Crosses Farm
....	Crosses Green
Dean Cottage	Dean House Coachmans Cottage
Dean Head	....
Dean Wood	....
Dry Field Lane	....
....	Ellers Farm
....	....
....	....

(1841)	(1851)
....	Finch Land Farm
Fir Hill	....
....	Fisher Houses
....	....
Gills	Gills Farm
Great House	Great House Farm
Great House Cottage	....
Green	....
Grut	Grut Farm
....	....
....	....
Hamers	Hamers Farm
Haslems	....
....	Higher Darbyshires
Higher House	Higher House
Higher Knowl	Higher Knoule
....	....
Intack	Intack Farm
Jepsons	Jepsons Farm
Kays Cottage	....
Knowl Bleach Works	Knowle Bleach Works
....	....
....	Latham Cottages
Lathams	Latham Farm
....	....
....	....
Lower Darbishires	Lower Darbyshires
Lower House	Lower House Farm
Lower Knowl	Lower Knoule
Marshs Cottage	....
Mather Hillock	Mather Hillock
Mill Hill	....
....	Moor Bottom Cottage

(1871)	(1891)
....	....
....	....
Fisher House	Fisher House
Gillsbrook Cottage	Gilsbrook House
....	....
Great House	Great House and Cottage
....	....
Greens Farm	....
Gruft	Grutt The
....	Hale Dairy
....	Hamers Cottage
Hamers	Hamers
....	....
Higher Derbyshires	Higher Darbyshires
Higher House	Higher House
Higher Knowle	Higher Knowle
Howarths Cottages	....
Intak	Intack
Jepsons	Jepsons Farm
....	Kays Cottage
....	....
....	Lakeland Villas
....	....
Lathams	....
....	Liverpool Waterworks
....	Lodge Gate House
Lower Derbyshires	....
Lower House	....
Lower Knowle	Lower Knowle
....	....
....	....
Mill Hill	Mill Hill
Moor Bottom	....

(1841)	(1851)
....	Moor Edge Cottage
Morris House	Morris House
New Hall	New Hall
....	....
Old Georges	Old Georges
Old Hall	Old Hall Cottage
Old Hall Farm House	....
....	Old Hallurells
....	Old Hills
....	Old Isaacs Farm
Old Cates	Old Kates Farm
....	Old Kiln
Old Knowl	Old Knowls Farm
....	....
Old Moses	Old Moseses
....	....
Old Rackets	Old Rachels Farm
Old Thatch	Old Thatch
....	....
Pall Mall	Pall Mall Cottages
Rivington Parsonage	Parsonage House
Pilkingtons	Pilkingtons Farm
....	....
Prospect	Prospect
Red Cat	....
....	Rivington
....	Rivington Hall
....	....
....	....
Sales Dean Head	Sales Farm and Cottage
School Brow	School Brow
School Cottage	School Cottage
....	School Houses

(1871)	(1891)
....	More Edge
Morris House	Morris House
New Hall	New Hall Farm
....	Nilcocks
Old Georges	....
....	....
....	....
Old Halliwells	Old Halliwells
....	....
Old Isaacs	....
Old Rates	Old Kates
Old Kiln	Old Kiln
Old Knowes	....
....	Old Mores
....	....
Post Office	Old Post Office
Old Rachels	Old Rachels
....	Old Thatch
Old Wills	....
Pall Mall	Pall Mall Cottages
Pasonage	Parsonage
Pilkingtons	Pilkingtons
Pilkingtons Cottage	....
Prospect	Prospect
....	....
Rivington	Rivington
Rivington Hall	Rivington Hall
Rivington Lodge	Rivington Lodge
Rivington Dairy	....
Sales and Cottage	....
School Brow	School Brow
....	School Cottage
....	Schoolhouse

(1841)	(1851)
....	....
Sheephouse Cottage	Sheephouse Cottage
Sheephouse Farm	....
Simms	Simms
Smith House	Smith House
Smithy Cottage	....
....	Sparth Farm
Spring Cottage	Spring Cottage
Stoaps	Stopes Farm
Street Bottom	Street Bolton Farm
Sweetloves	Sweetloves Farm and Cottages
....	Top oth Hill
....	....
Twig	Top oth Twig
....	Turners Cottage
Turners	Turners Farm
Wards	Wards Farm and Cottage
Watergate	Water Hey Cottage
....	....

(1871)	(1891)
Shant Stores	....
Sheep House	Sheephouse
....	Sheephouse Lane
....	Simms
....	....
....	....
....	....
Spring Cottage	Spring Cottage
Stopes	....
....	....
Sweetloves	Sweetloves
Top of the Hill	Top oth Hill
....	Top oth Meadows
Top of the Twig	Twig, The
....	....
Turners	....
Wards	Wards, Wards Cottage
Water Hdy	....
Wilcoks	....

FARM NAMES

FROM CARTOGRAPHIC RECORDS

THE FIRST EDITION 6-INCH MAP (1849)

The First Edition 6-inch Ordnance Survey Map of Lancashire, published in 1849, shows the landscape of Rivington and Anglezarke prior to the building of the reservoirs. Anglezarke and the upper portion of Rivington are detailed on sheet 78, and the remainder of Rivington on sheet 86.

The footnote to each sheet reads as follows:

SHEET 78

Surveyed in 1845-7, by Captain Tucker and Lieut. Stanley, and Bayly, R.E. Contoured in 1848, by Lieut. Barlow, R.E. and Engraved in 1848 under direction of Captain Yolland, R.E. at the Ordnance Map Office, Southampton, the Outline by E. May, the Writing by C. Darling, the Ornament by J. Hall, and Published by Lt. Colonel Hall, R.E. Superintendent, June 30th, 1849.

SHEET 86

Surveyed in 1845-7, by Captains Tucker, Hamley, Stanley & Bayly, R.E. Contoured in 1848, by Lieut. Barlow, R.E. and Engraved in 1848, under direction of Captain Yolland, R.E. at the Ordnance Map Office, Southampton, the Outline by W. Singleton, the Writing by J. Hutchison, the Ornament by George Rule, and Published by Lt. Colonel Hall, R.E. Superintendent, August 15th, 1849.

The list that follows does not include every farm or building detailed on each sheet, but only those within certain boundaries that I marked out on foot over the past half decade. These boundaries are roughly equal to the parish borders of Rivington and Anglezarke, albeit extending significantly to the north and east to include areas of Heapey and Withnell moors, the region to the west of Belmont Road (A675), and the small annex of woodland that contains the ruins of Hollinshead Hall.

NOTES

1   Dates in brackets indicate when the area was surveyed.
2   Italicised entries indicate a farm that is marked but not named. In these cases the name has been obtained by cross-referencing with the first edition 25-inch map.

SHEET 78
(1849)
Abbot's, Alance, Albion Villa, Anderton's, Batley Cabin, Botany Bay, Bradley's, Bromiley, Brook House, Brown Hill, Butter Cross, Calico Hall, Coomb, Coppice Stile House, Drinkwater's, Fir, Foggs, Goose Green, Great Hill Farm, Grimes', Hatch Place, *Heapey Moor Farm*, Heatons, High Bullough, Higher Hempshaw's, Higher House, Hill Top, Hollinshead Hall, Jepson's, Latham's, Lee House, Leigh Place, Liptrots, Lister Mill, Lower Hempshaw's, Lower House, Margery's Place, Marsdens, Moor Edge, Morris House, Moses Cocker's, Naylor's, New Ground, New Temple, Old Brooks, Old Isaac's, Old Kate's, Old Knowles, Old Rachel's, Parson's Bullough, Peewet Hall, Piccadilly, Pilkington's, Pimms, Ratten Clough, Sharrock's, Sheep House, Sheep House Farm, Siddow Fold, Simm's, Solomon's Temple, Sour Milk Hall, Sparks, Stone's House, Stoops, Sweetloves, Top o' th' Wood, Turners, Ward's Cote, White Hall, Whittles, *Wilcock's Farm*, Wilkinson Bullough.

SHEET 86
(1849)
Ainsworth's, Blackamoor's Head, Clump, Croft Gate, Crosse's,
Crosse's Coppice, Crosse's Green, Fir Hill, Fisher House, Gills,
Great House, Grut, Hamer's, Higher Derbyshire's, Higher Knoll,
Higher Ward's, Intack, Jepson's, Lower Derbyshire's, Lower
Knoll, Middle Derbyshire's, Mill Hill, New Hall, Old George's,
Old Thatch, Old Will's, Pall Mall, Parsonage House, Prospect,
Rivington Lodge, School Brow, Simm's Farm, Smith's House,
Spring Cottage, Top o' th' Hill, Top o' th' Meadows, Vale Cottage,
Ward's Farm.

THE FIRST EDITION 25-INCH MAP (1894)

The First Edition 25-inch Ordnance Survey Map of Lancashire was published in 1894. The following list is compiled from the various sheets which cover the Anglezarke and Rivington area.

NOTES

1. Dates in brackets indicate when the area was surveyed.
2. Italicised entries indicate a farm that is marked but not named. In these cases the name has been obtained by cross-referencing with the first edition 6-inch map.

SHEET LXXXVI-6
(1892)
Grutt Farm, Hamer's Farm, Jepson's Farm, Lower Knoll, Old Wills, Rivington Lodge.

SHEET LXXXVI-2
(1892)
Ainsworths, Beech House, Clump, Crosse's Green Farm, Crosses, Gilsbrook, Great House Farm, Higher Knoll, Higher Derbyshires, Higher Ward's Farm, Intack, Middle Derbyshires, Old Georges, Pall Mall, Prospect Farm, Rivington Hall, Rose Cottage, Simms Farm, Spring Cottage, Summerfield, Top o th' Hill Farm, Ward's Farm, Waterhey Cottage.

SHEET LXXXVI-1
(1892)
Blackamoor's Head Hotel, Chapel House, Croft Gate, Fisher House, Mill Hill, Parsonage House, School Brow.

SHEET LXXVIII-15
(1892)
Hill Top.

SHEET LXXVIII-14
(1892)
Bradleys, Brown Hill, *Coomb*, Crambo Cottage, Higher House, *Latham's*, Lower House, Moor Edge, Morris House, Moses Cockers, Old Kate's, *Old Knowles*, Old Rachel's, Sheep House, *Stoops*, Sweetloves, Wilcock's Farm.

SHEET LXXVIII-13
(1892)
Andertons, Dean Wood House, New Hall, Parson's Bullough, Pilkingtons, Rose Cottage.

SHEET LXXVIII-11
(1892)
Bromiley, New Barn, Ward's Cote.

SHEET LXXVIII-10
(1892)
Abbots, Foggs, Higher Hempshaw's, Lower Hempshaw's, Old
Brooks, Simms, Wilkinson Bullough.

SHEET LXXVIII-9
(1892)
Brook House, Jepson's Farm, Lee House, Manor House, Peewet
Hall, Siddow Fold, Stone's House.

SHEET LXXVIII-7
(1891)
Naylors.

SHEET LXXVIII-6
(1892)
Drinkwaters, Great Hill Farm, Grimes, Heapey Moor Farm.

SHEET LXXVIII-5
(1892–3)
Albion Villa, Coppice Stile House, Heapey Cottage, Margery's
Place.

SHEET LXXVIII-3
(1891)
Hollinshead Hall, Piccadilly.

SHEET LXXVIII-2

(1891–2)

Hatch Place, New Temple, Pimms, Ratten Clough, Solomon's Temple, Summer House, White Hall, Whittles.

SHEET LXXVIII-1

(1892)

Calico Hall, Fir Farm, Goose Green, Heatherlea, Heaton House Farm, Leigh Place, Liptrot's Farm, Marsden's Farm, New Ground, Sharrocks, Sour Milk Hall, Top o th' Wood (Blackhurst).

A DIGEST

6-inch Map (Sheet No)	25-inch Map (Sheet No)
Abbot's (78)	Abbots (LXXVIII-10)
Ainsworth's (86)	Ainsworths (LXXXVI-2)
Alance (78)	....
Albion Villa (78)	Albion Villa (LXXVIII-5)
Anderton's (78)	Andertons (LXXVIII-13)
Batley Cabin (78)	....
Blackamoor's Head (86)	Blackamoor's Head Hotel (LXXXVI-1)
Botany Bay (78)	Summer House (LXXVIII-2)
Bradley's (78)	Bradleys (LXXVIII-14)
Bromiley (78)	Bromiley (LXXVIII-11)
Brook House (78)	Brook House (LXXVIII-9)
Brown Hill (78)	Brown Hill (LXXVIII-14)
Butter Cross (78)	....
Calico Hall (78)	Calico Hall (LXXVIII-1)
Clump (86)	Clump (LXXXVI-2)
Coomb (78)	*No name* (LXXVIII-14)
Coppice Stile House (78)	Coppice Stile House (LXXVIII-5)
Croft Gate (86)	Croft Gate (LXXXVI-1)
Crosse's (86)	Crosses (LXXVXI-2)
Crosse's Coppice (86)	....
Crosse's Green (86)	Crosse's Green Farm (LXXXVI-2)
....	Dean Wood House (LXXVIII-13)
Drinkwater's (78)	Drinkwaters (LXXVIII-6)
Fir (78)	Fir Farm (LXXVIII-1)
Fir Hill (86)	Chapel House (LXXXVI-1)
Fisher House (86)	Fisher House (LXXXVI-1)
Foggs (78)	Foggs (LXXVIII-10)
Gills (86)	Gilsbrook (LXXXVI-2)
Goose Green (78)	Goose Green (LXXVIII-1)
Great Hill Farm (78)	Great Hill Farm (LXXVIII-6)
Great House (86)	Great House Farm (LXXXVI-2)
Grimes' (78)	Grimes (LXXVIII-6)

6-inch Map (Sheet No)	25-inch Map (Sheet No)
Grut (86)	Grutt Farm (LXXXVI-6)
Hamer's (86)	Hamer's Farm (LXXXVI-6)
Hatch Place (78)	Hatch Place (LXXVIII-2)
....	Heapey Cottage (LXXVIII-5)
Heapey Moor Farm (78)	Heapey Moor Farm (LXXVIII-6)
Heatons (78)	Heaton House Farm (LXXVIII-1)
High Bullough (78)	Manor House (LXXVIII-9)
....	Heatherlea (LXXVIII-1)
Higher Derbyshire's (86)	Higher Derbyshires (LXXXVI-2)
Higher Hempshaw's (78)	Higher Hempshaw's (LXXVIII-10)
Higher House (78)	Higher House (LXXVIII-14)
Higher Knoll (86)	Higher Knoll (LXXVXI-2)
Higher Ward's (86)	Higher Ward's Farm (LXXXVI-2)
Hill Top (78)	Hill Top (LXXVIII-15)
Hollinshead Hall (78)	Hollinshead Hall (LXXVIII-3)
Intack (86)	Intack (LXXVXI-2)
Jepson's (78)	Jepson's Farm (LXXVIII-9)
Jepson's (86)	Jepson's Farm (LXXVIII-6)
Latham's (78)	*No name* (LXXVIII-14)
Lee House (78)	Lee House (LXXVIII-9)
Leigh Place (78)	Leigh Place (LXXVIII-1)
Liptrots (78)	Liptrot's Farm (LXXVIII-1)
Lister Mill (78)	....
Lower Derbyshire's (86)	....
Lower Hempshaw's (78)	Lower Hempshaw's (LXXVIII-10)
Lower House (78)	Lower House (LXXVIII-14)
Lower Knoll (86)	Lower Knoll (LXXXVI-6)
Margery's Place (78)	Margery's Place (LXXVIII-5)
Marsdens (78)	Marsden's Farm (LXXVIII-1)
Middle Derbyshire's (86)	Middle Derbyshires (LXXXVI-2)
Mill Hill (86)	Mill Hill (LXXXVI-1)
Moor Edge (78)	Moor Edge (LXXVIII-14)

6-inch Map (Sheet No)	25-inch Map (Sheet No)
Morris House (78)	Morris House (LXXVIII-14)
Moses Cocker's (78)	Moses Cockers (LXXVIII-14)
Naylor's (78)	Naylors (LXXVIII-7)
New Ground (78)	New Ground (LXXVIII-1)
New Hall (86)	New Hall (LXXVIII-13)
New Temple (78)	New Temple (LXXVIII-2)
Old Brooks (78)	Old Brooks (LXXVIII-10)
Old George's (86)	Old Georges (LXXVXI-2)
Old Isaac's (78)	....
Old Kate's (78)	Old Kate's (LXXVIII-14)
Old Knowles (78)	*No name* (LXXVIII-14)
Old Rachel's (78)	Old Rachel's (LXXVIII-14)
Old Thatch (86)	Summerfield (LXXXVI-2)
Old Will's (86)	Old Wills (LXXXVI-6)
Pall Mall (86)	Pall Mall (LXXXVI-2)
Parson's Bullough (78)	Parson's Bullough (LXXVIII-13)
Parsonage House (86)	Parsonage House (LXXXVI-1)
Peewet Hall (78)	Peewet Hall (LXXVIII-9)
Piccadilly (78)	Piccadilly (LXXVIII-3)
Pilkington's (78)	Pilkingtons (LXXVIII-13)
Pimms (78)	Pimms (LXXVIII-2)
Prospect (86)	Prospect Farm (LXXXVI-2)
Ratten Clough (78)	Ratten Clough (LXXVIII-2)
Rivington Hall (86)	Rivington Hall (LXXXVI-2)
Rivington Lodge (86)	Rivington Lodge (LXXXVI-6)
Sharrock's (78)	Sharrocks (LXXVIII-1)
School Brow (86)	School Brow (LXXXVI-1)
Sheep House (78)	Sheep House (LXXVIII-14)
Sheep House Farm (78)	Rose Cottage (LXXVIII-13)
Siddow Fold (78)	Siddow Fold (LXXVIII-9)
Simm's (78)	Simms (LXXVIII-10)
Simm's Farm (86)	Simms Farm (LXXXVI-2)

6-inch Map (Sheet No)	25-inch Map (Sheet No)
Smith's House (86)	Beech House (LXXXVI-2)
Solomon's Temple (78)	Solomon's Temple (LXXVIII-2)
Sour Milk Hall (78)	Sour Milk Hall (LXXVIII-1)
Sparks (78)	Crambo Cottage (LXXVIII-14)
Spring Cottage (86)	Spring Cottage (LXXXVI-2)
Stone's House (78)	Stone's House (LXXVIII-9)
Stoops (78)	*No name* (LXXVIII-14)
Sweetloves (78)	Sweetloves (LXXVIII-14)
Top o' th' Hill (86)	Top o th' Hill Farm (LXXXVI-2)
Top o' th' Meadows (86)	Rose Cottage (LXXXVI-2)
Top o' th' Wood (78)	Top o th' Wood (LXXVIII-1)
Turners (78)	....
Vale Cottage (86)	Waterhey Cottage (LXXXVI-2)
Ward's Cote (78)	Ward's Cote (LXXVIII-11)
Ward's Farm (86)	Ward's Farm (LXXXVI-2)
White Hall (78)	White Hall (LXXVIII-2)
Whittles (78)	Whittles (LXXVIII-2)
No name (78)	Wilcock's Farm (LXXVIII-14)
Wilkinson Bullough (78)	Wilkinson Bullough (LXXVIII-10)

THE BOOK

MISCELLANEOUS NOTES ON RIVINGTON AND
DISTRICT FARMS AND OTHER BUILDINGS

The following transcript is taken from a photocopy of the book held at Bolton Library Local Studies Unit. The manuscript was deemed to be so delicate that the librarian made two copies, one of which was to be shelved and used in lieu of the original.

The book is a loose-leaf collection of 22 unnumbered, roughly A4-sized pages, with a 23rd written in pencil on a folded-out envelope. Most of the pages are type-written, but there are also pencilled additions, which are notated in the following transcription by [square brackets].

All original spelling, grammar and punctuation has been preserved, as has the page sequence. Bracketed ellipses (...) have been used to indicate portions of the text where the handwriting is illegible.

1 WILCOCK'S FARM [(BUTTER CROSS)]

Occupied in 1936. Until recently the date stone had been covered over by a porch stone. It reads

W A	R E
17	1670

The barn has a stone as follows:

W

T L B

1745

This is in raised characters, but incised between the letters and date is the date 1863. A corbel stone over the barn door reads

L

W. ^

1788

and another date inverted appears on a window cill 1787.

The present tenant removed here from Manor House. He went to Manor House in 1912 and remember[s] that Fogg's and Old Rachel's were inhabited shortly before that date. He stated that the stones which formed Brown Hill were removed to make or repair one of the reservoirs. The contractors running a line and bogeys to carry stones.

2 MORRIS HOUSE

The house has gone but the barn remains and is in use.

There was an Obadiah Morris of Anglesark in the 18th century.

3 ALANCE

This farm appears to be under the Yarrow reservoir and a new
Alance bridge built further east when the reservoir was made.

4 PARSON'S BULLOUGH

House demolished. Probably used for building the Yarrow
Reservoir, 1868–1875.

Barn in good state of preservation and in use.

5 STONES HOUSE

House in complete ruin. Barn in bad repair but used for housing implements. Raspberry canes in the old garden. The quarry had probably worked away considera[b]le land which went with this house.

In 1712 Roger Thropp, of Stone House in Anglesark was churchwarden at Rivington.

In 1772–3 'Thomas Grundy, for Stones House'.

6 JEPSON'S

Inhabited in 1936. House may have been rebuilt.

In 1704, churchwarden at Rivington was 'Thomas Mather, of Jepson's in Anglesark'.

7 HIGH BULLOUGH

Now known as Manor House. Probably been largely rebuilt.

Tablet in Rivington Church to George Shaw, Gentleman, fourth son of Lawrence Shaw of High Bollough, who gave in his lifetime £200 for a preaching minister at the church and left among other legacies £100, the profits thereof to be distributed amongst the poor inhabitants of Rivington, Andlesargh, Heath Charnock and Anderton on Peters Day and Michaels Day. Also £190 to be invested in land the profits thereof to form a fund wherefrom poor tenants may borrow.

Tablet to John Shaw, second son of Lawrence Shaw of High Bulhaugh in Anleyzargh, who left provision in lands whereby 10/- per annum for ever is to be paid towards the upkeep of Rivington Church and also the yearly sum of Twenty nobles to be distributed among the poor yearly forever on Good F[ir]days and the First Sunday in Advent.

Geor[a]ge Shaw died 8th November 1650, being 73 years of age.

John Shaw died 12th November 1627 being then 55 years of age.

8 PEEWET HALL

A complete ruin in 1936.

9 FOGG'S

Most of the roof had fallen in 1936. No striking features.

This farm had been inhabited up to about 1910.

10 ABBOT'S

In 1642 there was a 'Richard Abbott, husbandman, in Anglesarghe'. In 1696 a John Abbott of Anglezarke was church-warden at Rivington.

In a very ruinous state. Apparently not so large as some others.

11 WILKINSON BULLOUGH

In such a ruinous condition in 1936 that a large elder tree was growing up through the centre of the house.

A long house which had been added to, the barn being an extension to the house, as in the case of Old Rachels, Stoops and Coomb.

12 & 13 SIMM'S

Roger Simm, of Anglezarch, is referred to in 1731.

[In December 1936 this house and barn are in better (...) than any of the other ruined farms about here. The only sign of a date was in the barn, on a wooden beam which had supported the barn porch. The date read 1649. (?) A sketch plan of the buildings and house appears below.]

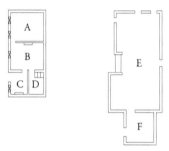

[The only entrance to the house is via room C which is approximately 12' × 9', contains a small fireplace and has a flagged floor. Part of the bedroom above this has a floor still more or less intact. Room B has a large fireplace and one large window from which is a grand view of the Pike & Winter Hill, including the ruins of Old Rachels, Stoops & Brown Hill. The floor is flagged. Room A has no fireplace. It is about 18' × 18'. Room D was the larder, with steps leading down to the cellar beneath. In one corner a stone probably (...) a spring.

The upper storey appears to have been divided into two large bedrooms, corresponding to A and B & C + D below. The doorway between those (...) A & B was over the doorway below, whilst the doorway between B & C + D was above the cellar steps.

The (...) of the staircase was not apparent. At some time there had been a door into room B from the outside at the back of the house (...) a window in that side in room A. The old track was on that side of the house and in the barn E a side doorway on that side has been partially filled in, & a small doorway left. The big doorway in the south side had a porch, (...) to above. The garden to the house had been on the south side in the (...) and a pig sty with each (...) above was just outside the garden. F is a stable for 3 horses. The barn is built of small stones and the house of large stones set in mortar.

An unusual form of roof truss in the barn at Sims. The beam rests on the walls of the barn. The roof is of stone slabs.]

14 LOWER HEMPSHAWS

Ruinous in 1936, but remains of a staircase still visible.

Like Higher Hempshaws this also had a good barn. In the garden on the south side the stone edging of a flower bed was found overgrown with turf.

[The (...) the doorway may have held the date stone. The barn is very similar to that of Higher Hempshaws with brick floors to cow stalls. A pig sty also in the yard. The fireplace in the north end room, an addition to the main house, has stone supports roughly carved. There is also a very low stone bench in this room. House of stone set with mortar. Interior plaster made with (...) material and in partition walls sticks with the back on were used instead of (...)]

15 HIGHER HEMPSHAWS

Said to be a corruption of Helmshaws.

Had been a fine barn. House may have been two joined into one. Remains of a small close planted with trees which may have been a garden. [The grass (hue?) ſtands out green againſt the surrounding moorland.]

There was a hamlet of Helmeshawes in 1566. [The barn is separate from the house.

A ſtone in the left hand side of the farther gateway has the following incised inscription. The ſtone is rough and incision shallow & looks like the work of an amateur.

AF
1741

(...) has remains of ſtone slab partition and bricked cow ſtandings. A pig ſty is in the yard. There is also a kind of barn, or perhaps loom house, attached and under one (...) with the house.

The ſtone walls are set in mortar.]

16 STOOPS

A small cottage in ruinous condition, 1936, but the barn had been
in recent use.

17 OLD KNOWLES

Practically nothing left.

Referred to in 1765. 'William Latham, for Old Knowes'. Also 'James Bain for Old Knowl.' in 1844.

[There is the ruin of a barn at the south end and a small house adjoining it in the north. All built of small stone set in mortar with very large stones at all corners.]

A complete ruin in October 1936. [Nothing left except part of the walls now incorporated in fencing walls.]

Stone found in yard

> N
> I A
> 1734

John Nightingale. Was a trustee of the Nonconformist Chapel 1737. In 1776, John Nightingale of Brown Hill is again referred to.

In 1845 'James Bain, for Nightingale's. Anglezark'.

[Christopher Brownlow about 30 yrs.]

19 HIGHER HOUSE

A complete ruin in 1936. [Little left except a few feet of the outside walls and the end of a barn.]

20 COOMB

A ruin in 1936. ~~Appears to have been a large house but~~ said to
have been only one storey high. Originally part built of large
stone blocks laid dry. Addition had been made at different times.
Drinking place in yard protected by upright stone slabs. [The walls
of the dwelling house are a feet thick. A sheep-pen on the south-
west corner is still intact and may still be used, as sheep are grazed
on this land. The buildings appear to have been all under one roof
with the house. The stones used for the walls of the outbuildings
are small compared with the nicely squared large stones in the
house walls. A (...) adjoins the the house, the stone floor and one
upright slab for a partitition still remain also a stone shelf across
one corner and the usual type of ventilators in the wall – like
archers' windows. Some land on the Noon Hill side, opposite the
front of the house, had been under the plough and also some land
just above the quarry.

21 OLD RACHEL'S

Partly standing in October 1936.

A large open fireplace with ingle-nooks. A stone porch to front door with seats. Built lengthways into the side of the hill. [The barn, built on the end of the house, had been a large one.]

Was occupied in 1841 by Roger Brown, who was churchwarden.

Old Rachels and Abbotts were inhabited until about 1910.

C
RAM
1693.

Cocker, Robert, wife, and Moses, son.

Moses, one of 'the four pious men' who seceded from the
Unitarian Chapel about about 1760 and founded the cause which
developed into Lee Chapel.

Occupied, October 1936.

23 APPENDIX

Rivington Park presented to (Corpn?) of Bolton by WH Lever of Thornton Hough in Wirral laid out & present Lord of Manor in 1904, (360 acres) : Bolton has nature (...) : Veins of lead & (calamine?) formerly worked : ancient mound of noon hill. Beacon said to mark portion of one older mentioned 1591. Lever acquired manor & estate in 1900, includes 2,100 acres 1902 L'pool Corpn sought to & finally succeeded (to buy?) all the land to preserve purity of water supply; own the soil of park, but have to maintain it.

Rivington Hall orig wood & plaster in [ ], none remains except [ ] form : house part rebuilt end 17 or early 18 century upper part of wing later : greater part rebuilt 1774 & (west?) part rebuilt.

Very fine old Barn 105' 8" long × 25' 6" wide main span (aisles recently added & now = 57' 6" wide) 6 (...) make it 7 bays. porches & roof also new tea house.

Great House Farm probably middle 17th cent : fine old farm, remains restored tea house one time much larger – also = fine specimen ancient timber construction as does Old Barn (date 1702 – date of repair some repairs).

Anglezarke – No village, but hamlet of White coppice & Hempshaws : Lead was formerly worked, referred to in 1694. Standishes of Duxbury (with others) had estates there.

NOTES

1. **VALLEY OF THE SMALL RIVER** : Written in Lancashire between 2005 and 2008. First published as *Landings*, 2009, Sustain-Release Private Press.

3. **ANGLEZARKE** : Text adapted from *The Victoria History of the County of Lancaster*, VOLUME V, 1911.

Anglezarke comprises the most westerly edge of the West Pennine Moors in southern Lancashire, UK. It is bounded to the north by Heapey, Wheelton and Withnell moors, to the east by Longworth, Turton and Darwen moors, and to the south by Rivington Moor and the River Yarrow, which descends from the hill known as Will Narr.

The name itself, like those of the deserted farms on its low hills, is enigmatic, allusive, hermetic. Current scholarship leans towards a Norse-Gaelic etymology. The first part of the word, *Anglez*, is thought to refer to a personal name, commonly held to be Anlaf, which itself is derived from the popular Scandinavian name Oláfr. Historically, Norse settlers are thought to have come to this region from Scotland, the west coast of Ireland, or possibly the Isle of Man, during the 9th or 10th century.

The second part, *arke*, had a more complex history. It is believed to be a form of the Middle English *ergh* or *argh*, found as the Gaelic loan-word *erg* in Old Norse, and ultimately derived from the Gaelic *àiridh*.

Some Irish-Gaelic references:

Àiridh (better *àirigh*), Hill pasture, shieling (*airghe*, in Lh. for Gaelic); cf. Early Irish *airge*, *áirge*, place where cows are, dairy, herd of cattle; Early Irish *airgech*, herdswoman of Brigit; Irish *airghe*, pl. *áiríghe*, a herd of cattle; *airgheach*, one who has many herds; **ar-egia*; Latin *armentum*? But see *àrach*, rear. Norse or Danish *erg* from Gaelic equals Norse *setr* (Ork. Sag.). This Norse form proves the identity of Gaelic with Early Irish *airge*; *airge=ar-agio*, **agio*, herd.

(*An Etymological Dictionary of the Gaelic Language*, Alexander MacBain, 1911)

These Scottish-Gaelic definitions are also of interest:

Aire, s.f. (Ir. *aire*.) Notice, regard, attention; thoughts, observation, watching. 'Thug iad aire dhomh', they gave me attention. 'Aire leagte air saoghail dhorcha', his thoughts fixed on worlds unknown. —Oss. Conn. 'Fo aire', under observation; in custody. —Oss. Fing. 'An ti a bheir an aire', he who regards or attends. —Stew. Pro. 'Gun aire dhomh', unknown to me; without my notice. 'Thoir an aire', take care. 'Ait aire', an observatory; 'tigh aire', an observatory; also a house where there is a corpse; a house where vigils are held over a corpse; Scotch, late-wake. 'Thoir an aire dhomh', attend to me.

Aireach, ich, s.m. (from *aire*.) A grazier; a keeper of cattle; a shepherd; a watchman. N. pl. *airichean*.

Aireach, a. (from *aire*.) Watchful, attentive, observant; sober; rarely hostile, violent. Comp. and sup. *airiche*, more or most watchful. — Stew. Tit.

Aireachail, a. (ie. *aireach-amhuil*.) Attentive, watchful, observant, circumspect.

Aireachas, ais, s.m. A pastoral life; tending cattle; the occupation of a shepherd; watchfulness.

Àiridh, s.m. A green grove; a place where osiers grow. 'Thig taibhse gu dian an àiridh', ghosts shall issue wildly from the osier meadow. — Oss. Temo.

Airidh, and *Airigh*, s.m. (perhaps *aire-thigh*.) A shealing; hill pasture; a mountain booth or hut; a shepherd's cottage. 'Thig do 'n airidh mo chailinn', come to the shealing, my maid. —Old Song. 'Bothan àiridh am braighe Raineach', a mountain hut in the braes of Rannoch; —the name of one of the finest Highland melodies; 'àiridh dhamh', pasture for oxen. —Stew. Is.

(*A Gaelic Dictionary*, R.A. Armstrong, 1825)

Although contemporary scholarship has disregarded some of

the ideas put forward by previous generations, it is interesting to reflect upon them nonetheless. In 1904, for example, W. M. Fergusson Irvine wrote:

> Anglezargh (Andelevesarewe, 1202; Anlauesargh, 1224) is a name evidently akin to Goosnargh, Skelmersargh, Ainsargh, Brettargh, and Grimsargh, and is said to contain in its last syllable a Norse word meaning a heathen temple. This has been disputed, but it is certainly curious that in two of the above, at least, the first portion of the name includes that of a Norse deity, an argument, however, which loses much of its force owing to the fact that names of deities were often taken as personal names by the early settlers. The name modernised would be Anlaf's-argh.

To these notes he added:

> Mr. Harrison writes to me: '*Argh*, or *hargh*, was certainly long thought to represent the Old Norse *hörg-r* = Old English *hearg*, a heathen place of worship or temple; but, although this signification is doubtless true as to, say, the Harrow, near London, some comparatively recent topographical researches by North Lancashire antiquaries seem to make it quite clear that the second element in place names such as Grimsargh and Goosnargh is a land-name, apparently meaning ploughed or harrowed ground; cf. Mid.-Dan. *harge*, Dut. *hark*, Swed. *harka*—a rake or harrow—all allied to Old Norse *herfi*, Dan. *harv*—a harrow. English *harrow*, Middle English *harwe*, is from an unrecorded Old English *hearg(e)*.'
>
> (*A Short History of the Township of Rivington*, W. M. Fergusson Irvine, 1904)

Shieling; pasture; grazier's land; a place of watchfulness; bothy; green grove; a place of worship; land under the plough; harrowed ground.

The name endured, at least, eluding exact definition. Meanings cluster the thin soil like nettles. One generation's flower may become another's weed.

In previous editions of *Landings*, attempts were made to reconstruct a narrative of 'Anglezarke' from various sources, giving the impression of linearity, stability, succession. But such is the diversity of different forms and dates of occurrence that the task is overwhelming, futile even. Moreover, as the sources of these references are not the original manuscripts, wills, deeds and memorial stones, but rather secondary texts written by historians, linguists, cartographers, etc., it is supposed that their faithfulness cannot be entirely guaranteed. Indeed, errors of transcription were doubtless introduced in compiling these very notes. Errors compounded upon errors, and so on.

What follows, therefore, is at best an incomplete list of instances of the word Anglezarke, in its different forms, cited in the works of others.

Andeleves *arewe*	1202	(1,4)
Anlaues *argh*	1224	(4)
Anlaues *argh*	1225	(1)
Anlewes *earche*	1246	(1)
Anlawes *aregh*	1246	(1,4)
Anlawes *arwe*	1246	(4)
de Anneles *herg*	1246	(4)
Anlase *harghe*	1285	(4)
Alase *harghe*	1288	(1)
Aneles *argh*	1292	(1)
Aneles *aregth*	1292	(1)
Anles *arath*	1292	(1)
Anles *aragth*	1292	(1)
Anlaghes *arghe*	1302	(1)
Anlas *argh*	1341	(4)
Anlas *argh*	1351	(1)
Anlaz *arghe*	1559	(1)

Anlez *argh*	1566	(8)
Anglez *argh*	1566	(2)
Anleyz *argh*	1627	(2,3)
Anglez *arke*	1628	(1)
Angles *arghe*	1642	(2)
Anlez *arke*	1647	(3)
Andles *argh*	1650	(2,3)
Anglez *argh*	1650	(3)
Anglez *argh*	1682	(3)
Anglez *argh*	1692-3	(3)
Anglez *arke*	1696	(2)
Anglez *argh*	1697	(3)
Anglez *ark*	1699	(3)
Angles *ark*	1704	(2)
Andles *ark*	1704	(7)
Anglez *ark*	1705-8	(7)
Anliz *ark*	1707	(7)
Anlez *ark*	1709-12	(7)
Anlisz *ark*	1713	(7)
Anlez *ark*	1713-28	(7)
Anglez *ark*	1715	(3)
Anlez *ark*	c. 1720	(3)
Anglez *ark*	c. 1720	(3)
Anglez *argh*	1727	(3)
Anlez *ark*	1730-56	(7)
Anglez *arch*	1731	(2)
Anlez *ark*	1733-7	(7)
Angliz *argh*	1738	(3)
Anlez *argh*	1739-41	(7)
Anlez *ark*	1743-4	(7)
Anlez *ark*	1752-8	(7)
Anglez *ark*	1757-1811	(7)

Anglez *ark*	1813-70	(7)
Angelz *ark*	1841	(5)
Anglez *ark*	1845	(2)
Anglez *arke*	1894	(6)

(1) *The Victoria History of the County of Lancaster*, VOL. V, Farrer & Brownbill, 1911.

(2) *Miscellaneous Notes on Rivington and District Farms and Other Buildings*, Anonymous, 1936.

(3) *A Short History of the Township of Rivington...*, W. M. Fergusson Irvine, 1904.

(4) *The Place-Names of Lancashire*, E. Ekwall, 1922.

(5) *Census Records Digest*, 1841.

(6) First Edition 25-inch *Ordnance Survey Map*, 1894.

(7) *Rivington Church Parish Records, Baptisms and Burials*, 1730-1870.

(8) *History of Rivington*, Thomas Hampson, 1893.

12. THE BOOK : Entitled *Miscellaneous Notes on Rivington and District Farms and Other Buildings*, 'the book' is a loose-leaf collection of observations about the material condition of various farms situated in, or around, the Yarrow valley. It describes twenty-one buildings in total:

Wilcock's Farm, Morris House, Alance, Parson's Bullough, Stones House, Jepson's, High Bullough, Peewet Hall, Fogg's, Abott's, Wilkinson Bullough, Simm's, Lower Hempshaws, Higher Hempshaws, Stoops, Old Knowles, Brown Hill, Higher House, Coomb, Old Rachel's and *Moses Cocker's.*

As might be intuited from its title, the tone is rather serious and somewhat detached. Nevertheless, there is something in the brevity of the descriptions contained therein; something in their matter-of-factness, which renders them poignant:

Old Knowles

Practically nothing left.

Referred to in 1765. 'William Latham, for Old Knowes'.

Also 'James Bain for Old Knowl' in 1844.

What emotions linger at the edges of those pages? What words unsaid? Or perhaps a certain kind of stoicism – of pragmatism – was in keeping with those times? Certainly, here is someone not simply remarking upon what is there. Here, rather, is someone trying to establish a context, a historical connection.

It is interesting to imagine these buildings in the first years after their abandonment.

The stone edging of a flower bed.

Raspberry canes in the old garden.

Perhaps they would have been oddly compelling, forbidding even, in their emptiness – in their isolation. Today, most of them are little more than piles of rubble, but in 1936 (the ostensible date of the book), a mere fifteen years since they were abandoned, there would surely have been a residual warmth, a lingering reminder of their last occupants.

13. MANY OF THESE PLACES HAVE NAMES : The question of names, name-giving and remembrance is a recurring one. What if we viewed toponymic evolution and mutation through the prism of the natural environment and its physical processes? Accretion. Attrition. Weathering (see *Rapture*, p. 71). If names become tangible, how do they gather around certain loci? How do they endure, or become transformed? Why is one tumble of stones still given the dignity of a name, when another has passed into anonymity? What is the link between the physical monument and its cartographic representation? If these stones could be shored up, somehow, would it defer the inevitable – their eventual unnaming?

Clearly, map makers are constrained by issues of scale, resolution and proportion, which may necessitate the omission of certain, finer-grained toponymic details. What at first might seem arbitrary may be the result of a reasoned, pragmatic process. But these omissions, whether accountable or not, are still losses. If the name of a farm, stream or wood is forgotten, then the stock of words that we use to engage with the landscape is diminished.

Maps are vital repositories of our knowledge of place. They enshrine the collective memory – recording not only what is current, but what is deemed worth holding onto from the past. But in so doing, they enforce a mononymous relationship between name and place – rarely does any location receive more than a single epithet. Yet this fact belies the complex relationship we have with our surroundings, and the many different ways in which we express our sense of belonging. Shouldn't there be room on maps for local names, folk-names and familial names; for narrative, personality and myth? What happened to the polyonymy of place?

I think back to the many notebooks I left in various corners of Anglezarke. Was I attempting to add materially to an environment that I felt was being eroded – to privately staunch the flow, to halt the perceived decline, to resuscitate, reinvigorate? Words literally tethered to places as others fall from the pages of maps. But, of course, in many respects my actions were futile. Over time, pages became fused together with water and earth; their contents rendered unreadable. Ultimately, I could only observe, reflect and simply bear witness to the process of decay.

13. OLD RACHEL'S : A compelling ruin on the south banks of the Yarrow. *The book's* author refers to it both with and without the apostrophe. Similarly, Abbot's is both Abbotts and Abotts. Simms is also Sims. These are perhaps trivial examples, but they serve to illustrate that the spelling of these

place-names was rarely standardised. More interestingly, Old
Knowles is written variously as Old Knowes and Old Knowl.

16. YARWE. EARWE. YAREWE. : Incanting the River Yarrow – the
southern border on which the moor rests. A threshold, a
liminal pathway, a place of meetings.

    Just as its physical source emanates from somewhere near
the hill ridge above the ruins of Hempshaws farm, so the
name source of the Yarrow is equally elusive:

Yarwe	1190
Earwe	1203
Yarewe	1246
arugh	1276
Yaro	1540
Yarowe	1577

    One possible derivation is from the Brittonic *arwā, in
which the first element, *ar, gives us the sense of 'starting up,
springing up, or setting in motion'. It is also plausible that
yarrow shares a common root with the little-used, Modern-
English word *yare* (Anglo-Saxon *gearu*, *gearo*), meaning
'ready, quick or prompt'. This can be traced through the
Old-English word *gearwe* (Anglo-Saxon *gearuwe*, *gearwian*),
which means 'that which prepares or sets in order'. And if
we also consider that curative plant of the same name (the
Common Yarrow, *Achillea millefolium*), then we get the sense
of 'to dress' (ie: to heal, from the Anglo-Saxon *gerwan*).

    Or perhaps the word is simply a corruption of *arrow*, from
the Old-English *ārwe*, and the Proto-Germanic *arhwō. A
metaphorical description? Flight of the river. And lastly, we
have the earthen, prosaic, Proto-Celtic *garwo (Welsh *garw*,
Irish *garbh*), meaning 'coarse' or 'rough'. In all, it is a word
with ambiguous origins, but perhaps there's a clue elsewhere
– in the landscape itself. There is more than a passing

connection between moor and river – between Andeleves–
arewe (1202), and Y–*arewe* (1246). An incidental similarity,
perhaps, but there is a resonance, nevertheless. *Two joined
into one.*

18.   SP : In the absence of anything more than the bare facts of
her life, as listed in the public record, SP is but a shadow
from the past. Like the nameless girl from the photograph
of Old Rachel's farm she is a ghost-figure. An armature on
which to hang the flesh of the imagination. During my time
on the moors I felt these two identities merge so that they
became aspects of each other – fragments of a diffuse and
shifting persona. But see notes to p. 159.

18.   NIÉPCE : Joseph Nicéphore Niépce, 1765–1833. Creator of
the heliographic process – the first successful example of
what later became known as photography.

19.   MEIKLE : Andrew Meikle, 1719–1811. Credited with the
invention of the threshing machine – an apparatus used to
separate grain from stalks and husks.

21.   HEMPSHAWS : Listed separately on the current Ordnance
Survey map as Higher Hempshaw's and Lower Hempshaw's.
For reasons hidden to myself now, I have always referred to
the two derelicts collectively as simply Hempshaws.

23.   SHELTER BELTS OF TREES : These plantations are a relatively
recent phenomena. Following Gladys Sellers, they are
described as shelter belts – corridors of conifers erected
to provide protection for subsequently planted mixed-
deciduous trees, which are intended to ultimately replace
them and thereby enrich the soil. There is much debate,
however, about the efficacy of such programmes and the
worth of monoculture woodland in general. There are also
suggestions that the recent proliferation of such plantations
has less to do with conservation and land improvement,

and more to do with economic benefits – in the form of tax-breaks and subsidies offered to stimulate the use of 'uncultivated' land.

30. TURNERS AND ALANCE : 'Alance Bridge' is actually named on maps prior to 1868, but like the farm from which it derived its name, it now lies ruined under many feet of water. A grander structure was erected further downstream, c.1877, spanning the much-widened river as it bled into the new reservoir.

30. THREE OTHERS : Accompanying these is another smaller reservoir, situated below High Bullough farm, which was built in the 1850s by the Chorley Waterworks Company. Subsequently decommissioned, it is now a protected area for wildlife, and the pathways by its banks have become nature trails that are popular with visitors.

It is interesting to observe the changing narrative of land use. An unintended by-product of these mid-Victorian-era civil engineering projects has been the creation of habitat for aquatic flora and fauna. Nature colonises without consent; with boundless disregard for design or utility. I think again of the ruined farms on the high moor:

> A lone foxglove grows between
> two collapsed roofing beams.
> Nettles gather around the blasted
> fireplace.
>
> (*Mirror* (p. 52))

These aren't shrines to the departed, but breeding grounds – places of rebirth and renewal. Did the Liverpool Corporation unwittingly help the landscape return to a more 'natural' state by protecting the Anglezarke water-catchment from the contaminants associated with human habitation? Has there been a consequent increase in the moor's biodiversity over the intervening years? And what about those landscapes where rural settlements disappeared under water – is that loss mitigated by the proliferation of new ecosystems? Is there some recompense to be found in the tenacity and fecundity of nature?

A provocative example is the valley of Haweswater, in Cumbria, which was flooded in the 1930s to provide water for the city and suburbs of Manchester over 70 miles away. Prior to the raising of the water level, the villages of Mardale Green and Measand were vacated, their buildings demolished and their dead exhumed and carried to the nearby village of Shap, where they were reinterred.

The valley is accessible today via a road skirting the south-east edge of the reservoir, and there is a hotel proudly advertising its location as 'set amongst 26,000 acres of unspoilt natural beauty'. At the moment of writing these notes the area has a celebrity visitor attraction in the form of a golden eagle. An almost extinct species in England, it is thought to have bred successfully in the valley since the late 1960s, although the current incumbent is a lone male. An RSPB reserve and monitoring station have been subsequently established, and it is hoped that the bird will eventually attract a mate.

It is not without irony that sites of rural depopulation such as Haweswater have become visitor attractions; havens that the general public flock to in order to escape the confines of the built environment. And what about Anglezarke? Its landscape is perhaps too subtle for mass appeal. As often as not during my time there I had the moors to myself – but despite my desire to connect, to understand, to give voice to the landscape, was I simply a visitor too? A tourist? And what about the notebooks, boxes and other artefacts that I

secreted about the moors – were they little more than litter?
No better than the plastic bottles, cans and other refuse that
are the most telling, and perhaps most enduring, legacy of
human visitation?

31. RIVINGTON WAS SPARED : Although certain limits were
placed on the Corporation's powers to acquire land, it was
still granted the inviolable right to 'protect' its water supply
on those lands that it didn't own:

> 13.2 In addition to all other rights and remedies the Corporation may
> possess for preventing the pollution of or interference with the waters
> flowing either directly or indirectly into the Rivington Waterworks
> they may at any time or times execute in or upon any lands or buildings
> in the drainage area of the said waterworks which by this section
> the Corporation are prohibited from acquiring otherwise than by
> agreement any works which may be necessary for the purpose of
> protecting from contamination fouling or discolouration the waters
> flowing directly or indirectly into their said waterworks.
>
> (*The Liverpool Corporation Act*, 1902)

33. Data from the 1901 Census records.

36. DEATH'S WITNESS : I.M. Louise Skelton, 1975–2004.

56. FAIERLOKKE : Eilert Ekwall, in *The Place-names of
Lancashire*, quotes *Faierlokke* as an alternative name cited
by Leland for Rivington Pike; a popular hill summit to the
south of Anglezarke Moor. Ekwall suggests that Rivington is
derived from the Old English *hrēof* 'rough, rugged', although
other writers prefer *rowan*, referencing the rowan tree or
mountain ash, possibly due to the earlier spelling Rowinton.

Interestingly, Ekwall, writing in 1922, used the form
Anglezark, whereas Farrer & Brownbill, writing in 1911, used
the form Anglezarke, in their *Victoria History of the County
of Lancaster*. So it would seem that, even in the modern era,
place-names such as this are far from fixed.

60. LEFT AN OFFERING : The act of hiding objects in special places is an age-old custom. Many people have bestowed coins or precious items within holes in walls, inside hollow trees or beneath stones. These things are wish tokens. Petitions. Elements within private rituals. Despite the manifold intentions behind such gestures, the recipients of these gifts are rarely, if ever, other human beings. Instead they are exchanges with the genius loci. A communion with the land itself, through its supernatural agencies. In a secular context the effect of such offerings is often to imbue a place with a sense of identity. To create a memory. A feeling of attachment.

61. Data from the 1901 Census records.

71. WIND-HOVER : The kestrel, *Falco tinnunculus*. A totemic bird, sadly in decline over recent decades. Historically persecuted, especially by gamekeepers (although its food source is mainly rodents and small birds, rather than grouse and pheasants), it has always appeared to me as the very life of the moor; its weightless centre. See also Pariah (p. 73), and Made (p. 84).

72. A FAINT TRACE : Is there ever 'eventual silence' (p. 14)? When sounds recede below the threshold of hearing, perhaps they linger, nevertheless. Diminishing but never gone completely. Commingling with the residual undersong – the map and vessel of all melodies.

73. MATTER FOR THE CONSTRUCTION OF SONG : These small items, and many more like them, collected from various locations across Anglezarke Moor, being *of* the landscape, *are* the landscape. They disperse the moor, extending its borders, conjuring it through touch and through memory. They collude in the sound-making process simply by virtue of their presence – their significance – but they can also become

plectra, or sonic objects themselves.

73. VESCH : See *A New English-Russian and Russian-English Dictionary* by M. Golovinsky, 1913:

> *Vesch*, sf. thing, object, article.

See also:

> *Veschestvo*, sn. matter, substance, essence.

76. CHURCHWARDENS' ACCOUNTS : Quoted from *History of Rivington* by Thomas Hampson, 1893.

79. ADERYN CORFF : Literally *corpse bird* in the Welsh language, a folk-name for the barn owl, *Tyto alba*; the *watcher* from the poem *Caged* (p. 43). Welsh belongs to the Brittonic family of Celtic languages which were once spoken much more widely throughout the British Isles. It is thought that a form of Brittonic called Cumbric was spoken in Yr Hen Ogledd (the Old North – a region that would have incorporated Lancashire) in the early Middle Ages.

80. MACHINIC : An obscure form. Here the phrase machinic murmur simply means 'the sound of machines'.

83. Data from the 1901 Census records.

85. THIS ERGH : A Middle-English variant of *erg*, a shieling (see notes *Anglezarke*, p. 269).

89. I BELONG TO THE MOOR : Phoebe Hesketh lived in the village of Rivington for many years. There's a sense that the disembodied voice from this poem – with its request, not for repose, but to reside in the wind – joins with those other voices that hover over the moor: the constant polyphony of cries and murmurs, birdcalls and distant traffic, and the river's song itself.

93. CHURCH ROAD : Church roads, corpse ways or coffin paths were ancient pathways used by remote communities for transporting the dead to officially designated places of burial, known as mother churches, where they could be properly

interred. Thought to be precursors to public rights of way, these corpse roads sometimes traversed difficult terrain, crossing streams, ditches and other obstacles.

> 1777—John Shaw, chapel warden for Jepson's, Rivington, and Obadiah Morris, in Anglezark, the sum of 6s. 8d., received for burials.

Rivington Church, believed to be built on the site of a much older place of worship, was consecrated in 1541. The oldest monument in its graveyard is said to date from the early 17th century. How, we might wonder, did the occupants of those remote moorland dwellings make their funerary passage to the grave site? On the 1894 map, a more or less straight track runs from Old Rachel's, past Brown Hill and across Dean Head Lane to Anderton's farm, where it turns south by Dean Wood House and onwards into Rivington village. But a procession coming from Helmshawsyde would still have to cross the Yarrow by the 'ford' at the base of the steep gully below Stoops farm – a difficult enough passage for the individual traveller. I think again of John Rawlinson's enigmatic aside:

> Another story was of the young son of one of the farmers being told by an aged farm labourer to go quietly over one of the fields on the moor edge, because a lot of brave men are buried there.
>
> (*Of the Last Generation* (p. 54))

One plot of soil confers immortality, and another oblivion. Was there ever a heretic tradition in these parts? Are there potter's fields? Private, unmarked graves high on the moors? Is there a lineage back to Anlaf, to the Anglo-Saxons, to the ancient Britons? Are there subtler remains amongst the tumuli and chambered cairns?

285

LANDINGS : NAMES. DATES. GENEALOGIES.

101. NAMES. DATES. GENEALOGIES : Written in England and
Ireland between 2009 and 2011. First published in the
expanded *Landings*, 2011, Sustain-Release Private Press, to
coincide with the *Landings* exhibition at the Douglas Hyde
Gallery, Dublin.

108. ARK : from *A Glossary of the Lancashire Dialect* by John H.
Nodal and George Milner, 1875.

108. HIM SE YLDESTA : from *Beowulf* trans. by A. J. Wyatt, 1894.

109. BROG : from *A Glossary of the Lancashire Dialect* by John H.
Nodal and George Milner, 1875.

109. GLISK : from *A Glossary of the Lancashire Dialect* by John H.
Nodal and George Milner, 1875.

110: WILDERNESS : For 'wilderness', see p. 21. In Britain it is
thought that humans began to significantly transform their
environment, from 'wild' to 'cultivated', in the Neolithic
period.

115. I HAVE HEARD : from *Joan of Arc* by Robert Southey, 1796.

117. AIRE LEAGTE AIR SAOGHAIL DHORCHA : 'his thoughts
fixed on worlds unknown', from *A Gaelic Dictionary* by R.A.
Armstrong, 1825. See notes to *Aire* (p. 270).

118. AUÐN : From *An Icelandic-English Dictionary* by Gudbrand
Vigfusson, 1874:

> The Icelandic language, in old writers also called the Norse or the
> Danish (Noræna or Dönsk tunga), was spoken by the four great
> branches of the Scandinavian race who peopled the countries abutting
> on the Baltic, the Norsemen or Northmen, Swedes, Danes, and Goths
> (Norðmenn, Svíar, Danir, and Gautar), as well as by the inhabitants of
> those parts of Northern Russia which were then known by the name
> of Gardar.

Regarding *auðn*:

> *Auðn*, F. [*auðr*, ADJ.], a wilderness, desert; *auðn* Sinai, Stj. 300. Land
> which has no owner or is waste, uninhabited ; *bygðust þá margar*

auðnir viða, many wide waſtes were then peopled, Eg. 15; *alla auðn
landsins,* Fms. i.5, VIII. 33, Greg. 33: the *auðn* was claimed as a royal
domain; *konungr á hér a. alla í landi,* Fms. XI. 225; *um þær auðnir er
menn vilja byggja, þá skal sá ráða er a. á,* the owner of the waſte, N.G.L.
I. 125: different from *almenningr, compaſcuum* or *common.*

  2. More ſpecially a deserted farm or habitation; *sá bær hét síðan á
Hrappſtöðum, þar er nú a.,* Ld. 24; *liggja í a.,* to lie waſte, 96, Grág. II.
214, cp. 278.

  3. Deſtruction; *auðn borgarinnar* (viz. Jerusalem), Greg. 40, Rb. 332,
Ver. 43, Sd. 179 (where *auðnu,* f.); *riki mitt ſtendr mjök til auðnar,* is in
a ſtate of desolation, Fms. XI. 320, Bret. 68: insolvency, utter poverty,
Grág. I. 62.

  Compounds: *auðnar-hús,* N. deserted huts, on mountains or in
deserts, Grág. II. 158. *auðnar-óðal,* n. impoverished eſtates, Sks. 333.
auðnar-sel, N. deserted shielings, Orkn. 458.

123. BENTYN : From *The Manx Dictionary in Two Parts* by John
Kelly, 1866. Manx is the Gaelic language of the Isle of Man,
which, along with Irish and Scottish Gaelic, belongs to the
Goidelic family of Celtic languages.

    Although I have uncovered no evidence of a ſpecific Manx
influence on the place-names of this area, there is a subtle
Gaelic legacy evident in river names such as the Douglas,
and, of course, the Norse-Gaelic hybrid Anglezarke.

    Contemporary scholarship suggeſts that these traces
of Gaelic came via the Scandinavian influx into northern
England in the tenth century AD. These incomers are
thought to have come from weſtern Scotland, the Hebrides,
Ireland and the Isle of Man. (See Diana Whaley, *A Dictionary
of Lakeland Place-Names,* pp. XXI-XXIII.)

    As with the Scottish Gaelic quotes in *Landings,* these
borrowings from Manx are an imaginative, linguiſtic
connection with the places from which Anlaf and his people

might have come.

123. ASHLINS : From *The Manx Dictionary in Two Parts* by John Kelly, 1866.

124. ÜTIC, ÜTIC : W. Percival Westell's description of the stonechat's call, in his beautiful book, *British Nesting Birds*, 1910. Amongst the folk-names he lists are *Furze Hacker* and *Stonesmith*. Westell's book is also useful as it records the old latin names, some of which have been subsequently revised. Here the stonechat is *Pratincola rubicola*, whereas the RSPB currently prefers *Saxicola torquata*.

124. CLAGHAN-NY-GLEIEE : From *The Manx Dictionary in Two Parts* by John Kelly, 1866:

> (Manx>English) *Claghan*, s. a stone step to cross a river, a pavement,
> (Ir. *cloghan*) *-ny-cleigh*, s. a stonechatter, a white ear.

Also:

> (English>Manx) *Stonechatter*, s. claghan-ny-gleiee.

128. BRID : A dialect form of 'bird', from *A Glossary of the Lancashire Dialect* by John H. Nodal and George Milner, 1875.

133. BASSAGH : From *The Manx Dictionary in Two Parts* by John Kelly, 1866.

134. Data from *A Short History of the Township of Rivington...* by William Fergusson Irvine, 1904.

135. RIVINGTON ... PENETRATE : Quoted from *A Short History of the Township of Rivington...* by William Fergusson Irvine, 1904.

136. THE APPROPRIATION ... CONSTRUCTION : Quoted from A Landscape Strategy for Lancashire, Landscape Character Assessment by Lancashire County Council, and others, December 2000 (with minor amendments 2004).

139. DUB : A dialect word for a pool, of possible Gaelic origin:

> *Dobhar*, water, Ir. *dobhar*, E. Ir. *dobur*, W. *dwfr*, Cor. *dofer*, Br. *dour*,
> Gaul. *dubrum*, *dubro-n*, *dub-ro-*, root *dub*, deep, as in *domhain*, q.v.

> Cf. Lit. *dumblas*, mire, Lett. *dubli* (*do.*); Lit. *duburys*, a place with
> springs, *dumburỹs*; Ger. *tümpel*, a deep place in flowing or standing
> water. Hence *dobharchu* ('water-dog') and *dobhran*, the otter.
>
> (*An Etymological Dictionary of the Gaelic Language* by Alexander
> MacBain, 1911)

Eilert Ekwall, in *The Place-names of Lancashire*, notes that
Hawes Water in Silverdale used to be called Arnside Dub.

139. DUBH GLAISI, DU GLAIS : The *black water* is the River
Douglas, into which the River Yarrow flows. Ekwall cites a
Celtic etymology: Irish *dubh glaisi*, Welsh *du glais*; literally
black stream.

139. SWIFT : A reference to the River Ribble, with which the
Douglas eventually merges:

> *Rhe*, a root found in many languages, meaning swift, or to run. The
> names of many rivers, as Rea, Rye, Rey, Ribble, &c., are derived from it.
>
> (*The Survey Gazetteer of the British Isles*, J. G. Bartholomew, 1904)

139. ARROW : For a discussion of the etymology of the river-name
Yarrow, see pp. 277–8.

140. BOND : The chthonic connection with a particular place
made through burying a small musical instrument and later
exhuming it. A petition to, and collusion with, the subtle,
imperceptible agencies of the landscape.

141. LOOM HOUSE : As with many of the mosaic sequences
throughout *Landings*, these reclaimed fragments from the
book are an attempt to reconstruct meaning, to rediscover
beauty, from dereliction. The word *corruption* commonly
has negative connotations, but in linguistics it simply means
morphological change – the slow process of transformation
that words can undergo over centuries of usage.

Although the text of the book itself is fairly intact, the
buildings it describes are ruinous, and, moreover, their
decline has advanced in the 70 years since it was ostensibly

written. In a sense, *Loom's* fragmentary structure is a grammatical corruption of the text, a reimagining of its narrative in a ruinous state.

142. THEAW'RT ITH' CLIFTS OTH' ROCKS : From *The Song of Solomon in the Lancashire Dialect* by James Taylor Staton, 1859.

142. MONNY WATTERS CONNOT QUENCH LOVE : From *The Song of Solomon in the Lancashire Dialect* by James Taylor Staton, 1859.

143. ABBOT ... YEATES : This list is only partial and cannot claim to be entirely accurate. It is provided to give a sense, rather than a census, of the names of people who lived in Rivington and Anglezarke parish. Many of the names are clearly duplicates due to variations in spelling and errors of transcription.

Amongst the sources are the birth and death records of Rivington Parish Church, 1703 to 1877, and Rivington Chapel, 1734 to 1819, provided by the *Lancashire Online Parish Clerks Project:* www.lan-opc.org.uk.

149. I HAVE LAID ME DOWN : from *Joan of Arc* by Robert Southey, 1796.

151. WORD-HOARD : Written in Cumbria in 2015. This appeared as an 'afterword' in the previous edition of *Landings*.

159. SP : Over the years, the decision not to name SP, except by her initials, was a difficult one. In 2010 I wrote:

> And what about SP? The girl-ghost who haunts the pages of my notebooks. Surely her full name should be noted for the record, given my preoccupation with names, their loss and recovery? It would be an act of respectful commemoration – a dignified footnote to the history of the moors. But my instincts advise me otherwise. I feel protective of her anonymity, and, moreover, respectful of the privacy of her living relatives. The bare facts of her life, as listed in the public record, evoke nothing but pity and pathos. By naming her, I feel that I condemn her to that *small* existence, that brief span of years, that sorrowful death.

But, by not acknowledging her full identity, did I end up unwittingly turning her into a symbol for all those 'who passed by like ghosts'? More thoughts from the past:

> Nevertheless, doubts and inconsistencies remain. By not naming her, she is, in a sense, lost. Just as my footsteps on the moors caused unintentional damage to the ruins I wished to preserve, so my reticence has made me an accomplice in the process of decay and forgetfulness.

Nearly a decade later and my ideas are less conflicted. Perhaps these things just take their time to resolve. And so, although she was, and will remain, SP to me, she was also known as Susannah Pilkington, the daughter of James Pilkington and Ellen Brownlow, 1865–1887. The 'list of parts' is now a little closer to being complete.

159. NODAL & MILNER : *A Glossary of the Lancashire Dialect* by John H. Nodal and George Milner, 1875. See Appendices for a partial transcription of this text. For 'inherent poetry', see p. 109.

160. GERSINS : See Appendices, *Lancashire Dialect Terms – Of Farming*.

CHEMICAL MEMORIES

165. CHEMICAL MEMORIES : Written in the Scottish Borders in
2018.

175. LEASE : See Appendices, *Lancashire Dialect Terms – Of
Weaving, Cloth-Making, Etc.*

234. DIGEST : Compare this list of 115 buildings with the mere
33 marked on the current Ordnance Survey Explorer Map
(NO. 287), produced in 2004:

> Bradley's, Bromiley, Calico Hall, Coppice Stile House, Dean Wood
> House, Drinkwater's, Great Hill Farm, Higher Derbyshires, Higher
> Hempshaw's, Higher Knoll, Jepson's Farm, Knowle House, Liptrot's
> Farm, Lower Hempshaw's, Manor House, Middle Derbyshires,
> Moses Cocker's, Naylors, Old Rachel's, Parson's Bullough, Piccadilly,
> Pike Cottage, Pimms, Rivington Hall Barn, Siddow Fold, Simms,
> Solomon's Temple, Spring Cottage, Stone's House, Ward's Cottage,
> White Coppice Farm, Wilcock's Farm, Wilkinson Bullough.

Perhaps some of the disparity can be explained by issues of
scale – the modern map is 1-25,000, or 2½-inches to the mile,
whereas the older maps are 6-inches (1849) and 25-inches
(1894) to the mile, respectively. Is there a modern map of
equivalent scale to perform a like-for-like comparison? The
Explorer Series is the Ordnance Survey's most detailed
'leisure' product. As such it represents, in cartographic form,
the collective, toponymic memory of the farms of Rivington
and Anglezarke.

237. TOP O THE' WOOD : On the 25-inch map, the name
Blackhurst is also written near Top o th' Wood.

237. WARD'S COTE : The building referred to as Ward's Cote on
the 6-inch map is listed as New Barn on the 25-inch map. A
different building to the north-east, which isn't present on
the older map, is listed as Ward's Cote on the 25-inch map.
This is most likely an error on the later map.

242. WILCOCK'S : The text is accompanied by two small photographs of Wilcock's Farm.

　　The first edition 6-inch Ordnance Survey map details a cluster of buildings along Dean Head Lane, but only names two of them – Butter Cross and Latham's. By contrast, the first edition 25-inch map names only one – Wilcock's. By comparing the two maps it is clear that Wilcock's and Butter Cross were two distinct farms.

253. SIMM'S : The description of the roof is accompanied by a 14 × 8.5cm photograph with the caption: 'Photographed from below, in doorway between E & F'.

255. LOWER HEMPSHAWS : The text is accompanied by two small photographs – the first a close-up of Lower Hempshaws and the second taken from some distance, with the caption: 'Lower and Higher Hempshaws'.

256. HIGHER HEMPSHAWS : A single photograph accompanies the text with the following caption: 'Below is photo taken through the barn doorway to Lower Hempshaws'.

257. STOOPS : There is a photograph of 'Stoops, from the Hempshaws side with Winter Hill in background'.

260. HIGHER HOUSE : There is a small photograph, taken from a distance, of 'the ruins of Coomb below Winter Hill'.

262. OLD RACHEL'S : There are two small photographs – the first a close-up of a large fireplace piled with rubble, and the second looking down on Old Rachel's from the brow of the hill behind the farm, with the ruins of Higher and Lower Hempshaws in the far distance.

263. MOSES COCKERS : The text is accompanied by a single photograph of the house at Moses Cocker's.

INDEX

BROOKS, RIVERS & STREAMS

HILLS & HIGH GROUND

* For the farm of the same name, see *The Old Farms & Buildings*

MOORS, PASTURE & SHIELING

Moor	3, 8, 10, 12, 13, 14, 15, 17, 19, 20, 21, 37, 38, 41, 49, 51, 53, 54, 56, 62, 67, 69, 73, 78, 85, 88, 89, 90, 103-6, 108, 110, 111, 117, 119, 122, 123, 126, 128, 133, 135-8, 140, 153, 156, 169, 177
Anglezarke Moor	31, 58, 62, 110, 137-8
Darwen Moor	27
Heapey Moor	126
Longworth Moor	27
Rivington Moor	64, 135-8
Pasture	17, 41, 106, 110, 160
Bromiley Pastures	71, 133
Folds Pasture	34
Hordern Pasture	71
Sam Pasture	104
Shieling	69, 85, 167
erg	i, 106, 121
ergh	85

RESERVOIRS & WATER
WOODS & PLANTATIONS

BIRDS & BIRD SONG

TREES

FLORA, FAUNA & MINERAL

THE OLD FARMS & BUILDINGS

OTHER NOTABLE REFERENCES

BIBLIOGRAPHY

·   Anonymous, *Beowulf*, (translated by A. J. Wyatt), 1894
·   Anonymous, *Miscellaneous Notes on Rivington and District Farms and Other Buildings* (otherwise known as 'the book'), unknown date & binding
·   Armstrong, R. A., *A Gaelic Dictionary*, 1825
·   Bartholomew, J. G., *The Survey Gazetteer of the British Isles*, 1904
·   Birtill, George, *Heather In My Hat*, 1977
·   Brown, George Mackay, *The Collected Poems of George Mackay Brown*, 2005
·   Ekwall, Eilert, *The Place-Names of Lancashire*, 1972
·   Farrer, William & Brownbill, J., *The Victoria History of the County of Lancaster*, VOLUME V, 1911
·   Golovinsky, M., *A New English-Russian and Russian-English Dictionary*, 1913
·   Hampson, Thomas, *History of Rivington*, 1893
·   Hesketh, Phoebe, *A Box of Silver Birch*, 1997 ('A Box of Silver Birch' reproduced by kind permission of Stephen Stuart-Smith, Enitharmon Press)
·   Hughes, Ted, *Collected Poems*, 2003
·   Irvine, William Fergusson, *A Short History of the Township of Rivington in the County of Lancaster; With Some Account of the Church and Grammar School*, 1904
·   Kelly, John, *The Manx Dictionary in Two Parts*, 1866
·   Macbain, Alexander, *An Etymological Dictionary of the Gaelic Language*, 1911
·   Nodal, John H. and Milner, George, *A Glossary of the Lancashire Dialect*, 1875
·   Rawlinson, John, *About Rivington*, 1969
·   Sellers, Gladys, *Walks On the West Pennine Moors*, 1988
·   Smith, Malcolm David, *About Anglezarke*, 2002

- Southey, Robert, *Joan of Arc, Ballads*, Lyrics and Minor Poems, 1866
- Staton, James Taylor, *The Song of Solomon in the Lancashire Dialect*, 1859
- Thomas, R. S., *Collected Poems*, 1945–1990, 2000
- Various Authors, *West Pennine Moors Management Plan (2010–2020)*, 2010
- Vigfusson, Gudbrand, *An Icelandic-English Dictionary*, 1874
- Westell, W. Percival, *British Nesting Birds*, 1910
- Whaley, Diana, *A Dictionary of Lake District Place-Names*, 2006

THE RECORDINGS

The *Landings* Recordings:

·   Carousell, *Landings*, 2006 (SRL04)
·   Richard Skelton, *Landings*, 2009 (SRL14)
·   Richard Skelton, *Rapture (Reprise)*, 2011 (SRL21)

Related:

·   A Broken Consort, *Box of Birch*, 2007 (SRL07)
·   Clouwbeck, *A Moraine*, 2007 (SRL08)
·   A Broken Consort, *Crow Autumn (Part One)*, 2007 (SRL09)
·   A Broken Consort, *Crow Autumn (Part Two)*, 2009 (SRL12)
·   Richard Skelton, *Marking Time*, 2008/11 (SRL16)

Compilations:

·   Richard Skelton, *The Complete Landings*, 2011
    (A compilation of SRL04, SRL14 and SRL21)
·   A Broken Consort, *The Complete Crow Autumn*, 2011
    (A compilation of SRL09, SRL12 and unreleased recordings)

Lightning Source UK Ltd.
Milton Keynes UK
UKHW022212011119
352743UK00006B/287/P